ADVANCES OF PYTHON

THE ONLY BOOK FOR STUDENTS,INDUSTRY PROFESSIONALS,PROGRAMMERS IN PYTHON PROGRAMMING

NISHANTA RANJAN NANDA

Made with ♥ on the Notion Press Platform
www.notionpress.com

This book is dedicated to my Almighty Lord Jaggannath, My Parents, my wife ,son from whom i have stolen some valuable time to dedicate to this book

Contents

Foreword

I had spent 17 years in IT industry and academics and i though of what i have always wanted to provideto the society and finally i landed up with the book which took around 1.5 years to be completed and published which was my dream of being a Technical book author to show some path to the students , programmers and professionals .When me and Alok decided to bring up something in the form of a book which will cater to the all needs of the students, graduates,programmers and professionals -we had to take many considerations for chapters and real programs for the same.And almighty is great to show us the path though which we are able to complete such a wonderful piece of work for the society,we may live or die but our work will be memorised in the form of the book ,hope i am not boring you all !! Enjoy this book with Interest of Python in your minds -and i will be with you.

Preface

The demand for data science and AI professionals is set to surge and cross more than one million professionals by 2024.The top five roles are ML engineer, data engineer, data scientist, data architect, and DevOps engineer, and make up for 73% of all AI job openings in India.The motive behind this book is pretty clear that we are not going to bore you, but we will provide a better flow of learning of things of Advanced Python Programming.Those who think that programming is not for them or difficult - I assure you that after going through the book you will find that the book starts from basic things to advanced Python Implementations gradually step by step in Data Science ,Machine Learning(Project Included),Web applications, image processing,Desktop Applications,Scientific and numeric calculations .And not limited to those only now Artificial intelligence,Robotics,Hacking,Quantum Computing,Blockchain,automation testing using Robot Framework are the need of the hour.Hope our book will cater to all the needs.

Acknowledgements

I would acknowledge LORD JAGANNATH and my Parents (Niranjan Nanda,ManjuBharati Nanda)without whom i could have never been able to come to this world neither complete this book.My Father and Mother are the persons without them i am nothing and could not be recognised in this world so all credit goes to them.I am proud of them and hope they will find the best that would make them abosultely proud after publication of this book.

My inspiration is my grand father Pandit Govind Chandra Mishra - a President award winner,he is still having a good relationship with his pen and paper at the age of 86 and still writing books - so i got inspired from him about writing something in form of a book for the society.

I have to start by thanking my awesome wife, Sasmi.Yes I do agree and would like to say sorry as i spent more time in compiling the book and my wife Sasmi and son Nikhil always complained about those golden time i had spent for this book overnight and after my office hours tired and restless hours together with this book,thank you so much dear.

I acknowledge Alok for all his thoughts of necessary chapters which was included in the book to serve the students, professionals and Programmers.My sincere gratitude towards NotionPress publication,they understand the value of this book in reality and helped me.

I would love to say thanks to all my teachers,friends ,office colleagues

Prologue

.This book is having 325 pages currently:

This book has been divided into the following chapters and comprises of around**325 Pages with the following audience**

Chapter#	Details	Level	Intended Audience
Chapter-1	OOPs concepts Basics	Beginner	Students,Professionals,Programmers
Chapter-2	String Data Python	Beginner	Students,Professionals,Programmers
Chapter-3	Numeric data Python	Beginner	Students,Professionals,Programmers
Chapter-4	List Tuples Dictionaries	Advanced Beginner	Students,Professionals,Programmers
Chapter-5	Print all the output	Advanced Beginner	Students,Professionals,Programmers
Chapter-6	Control your Programs	Intermediate	Students,Professionals,Programmers
Chapter-7	Achieve Real Goal -Functions	Intermediate ,Expert	Students,Professionals,Programmers
Chapter-8	Modules of Python	Intermediate	Students,Professionals,Programmers
Chapter-9	Handle your Exceptions	Intermediate ,Expert	Students,Professionals,Programmers
Chapter-10	Input & Output	Advanced ,Expert	Programmers
Chapter-11	Machine Learning Practical	Highly Advanced	Programmers, Industry Level Professionals

Arranagement of Chapters and Level and Audience

Chapter1:
This chapter is about basic object oriented concept of Python and exception handling in Python.

Chapter2:
This chapter talks about string data and various operations on String Data .

Chapter3:
This chapter contents numeric data and its conversions to scalar

Chapter4:
This chapter is most important for programmers, professionals as it describes lists, tuples, dictionaries used in Data science .

Chapter5:
This is about printing output and file object variables in Python programming .

Chapter6:
This is all about if loop, for loop, while loop- all related to control statements used in Python Programming

Chapter7:
This is describing Functions in Python to achieve some real goals in world of Python programming

Chapter8:
String Modules and Regular expressions, security and CGI are described here in this chapter with all examples .

Chapter9:
Dedicated Exclusively for Exceptions and handling the exceptions in different paradigms.

Chapter10:
This chapter is all about Python IO file handling with complex data types like list and dictionaries along with Regular expressions .

Chapter11:

This bonus chapter is all about the practical implementation of cross validation technique in Machine Learning forData Science implementations

Contents

6.Example of Python I/O

12

Implemenation of ML...

Chapter 1

Introduction

1.1 What is Python?

Python is a high-level scripting language which is used for a wide variety of text processing, system administration, internet-related tasks and wide variety of applications. Unlike many similar languages, it is a core language which is very small and easy to code, while allowing the addition of modules to perform a virtually limitless variety of tasks. Python is a purely object-oriented language, and is available on a wide variety of platforms.

Python was developed in the early 1990's by Guido van Rossum at CWI in Amsterdam, and currently at CNRI in Virginia. The python is small, clean syntax and the thoroughness of the implementation of ideas like object-oriented programming, without eliminating the ability to program in a more traditional style. So python is an excellent choice as a first programming language without sacrificing the power and advanced capabilities that users will eventually need.

The pictures of snakes often appear on python books and websites, the name is derived from Guido van Rossum's favorite TV show, "Monty Python's Flying Circus".

1.2 The very Basics of Python

There are a few features of python which are different than other program-ming languages, and which should be mentioned early on so that subsequent examples don't seem confusing. Further information on all of these features will be provided later, when the topics are covered in depth.

Python statements do not need to end with a special character – the python interpreter knows that you are done with an individual statement by the presence of a newline, which will be generated when you press the "Return" key of your keyboard. If a statement spans more than one line, the safest course of action is to use a backslash (\) at the end of the line to let python know that you are going to continue the statement on the next line; you can continue using backslashes on additional continuation lines. (There are situations where the backslashes are not needed which will be discussed later.)

Python provides you with a certain level of freedom when composing a program, but there are some rules which must always be obeyed. One of these rules, which some people find very surprising, is that python uses in-dentation (that is, the amount of white space before the statement itself) to indicate the presence of loops, instead of using delimiters like curly braces ({}) or keywords (like "begin" and "end") as in many other languages. The amount of indentation you use is not important, but it must be consistent within a given depth of a loop, and statements which are not indented must begin in the first column. Most python programmers prefer to use an edi-tor like emacs, which automatically provides consistent indentation; you will probably find it easier to maintain your programs if you use consistent in-dentation in every loop, at all depths, and an intelligent editor is very useful in achieving this.

1.3 Invoking Python

There are three ways to invoke python, each with its' own uses. The first way is to type "python" at the shell command prompt. This brings up the

The three greater-than signs (>>>) represent python's prompt; you type your commands after the prompt, and hit return for python to execute them. If you've typed an executable statement, python will execute it immediately and display the results of the statement on the screen.

For example, if I use python's print statement to print the famous "welcome to Python world" greeting, I'll immediately see a response:

ft. print 'welcome to Python world' welcome to Python world

The print statement automatically adds a newline at the end of the printed string. This is true regardless of how python is invoked. (You can suppress the newline by following the string to be printed with a comma.)

When using the python interpreter this way, it executes statements immediately, and, unless the value of an expression is assigned to a variable (See Section 6.1), python will display the value of that expression as soon as it's typed. This makes python a very handy calculator:

ft. cost = 27.00

ft. taxrate = .075

ft. cost * taxrate 2.025

ft. 16+25+92*3

317

When you use python interactively and wish to use a loop, you must, as always, indent the body of the loop consistently when you type your statements. Python can't execute your statements until the completion of the loop, and as a reminder, it changes its prompt from greater-than signs to periods. Here's a trivial loop that prints each letter of a word on a separate line — notice the change in the prompt, and that python doesn't respond until you enter a completely blank line.

ft. word = 'the python'

ft. for i in word:

...print i

...

The p y t h o n

The need for a completely blank line is peculiar to the interactive use of python. In other settings, simply returning to the previous level of indentation informs python that you're closing the loop.

You can terminate an interactive session by entering the end-of-file character appropriate to your system (control-Z for Windows, control-D for Unix), or by entering

import sys sys.exit()

or

raise SystemExit at the python prompt.

For longer programs, you can compose your python code in the editor of your choice, and execute the program by either typing "python", followed by the name of the file containing your program, or by clicking on the file's icon, if you've associated the suffix of your python file with the python interpreter. The file extension most commonly used for python files is ".py". Under UNIX systems, a standard technique for running programs written in languages like python is to include a specially formed comment as the first line of the file, informing the shell where to find the interpreter for your program. Suppose that python is installed as /usr/local/bin/python on your system. (The UNIX command "which python" should tell you where python is installed if it's not in /usr/local/bin.) Then the first line of your python program, starting in column 1, should look like this:

#!/usr/local/bin/python

1.4. BASIC PRINCIPLES OF PYTHON

After creating a file, say myprogram.py, which contains the special comment as its first line, you would make the file executable (through the UNIX com-mand "chmod +x myprogram.py"), and then you could execute your pro-gram by simply typing "myprogram.py" at the UNIX prompt.

When you're running python interactively, you can instruct python to ex-ecute files containing python programs with the execfile function. Suppose that you are using python interactively, and wish to run the program you've stored in the file myprog.py. You could enter the following statement:

execfile("myprog.py")

The file name, since it is not an internal python symbol (like a variable name or keyword), must be surrounded by quotes.

1.4 Basic Principles of Python

Python has many features that usually are found only in languages which are much more complex to learn and use. These features were designed into python from its very first beginnings, rather than being accumulated into an end result, as is the case with many other scripting languages. If you're new to programming, even the basic descriptions which follow may seem intimidating. But don't worry – all of these ideas will be made clearer in the chapters which follow. The idea of presenting these concepts now is to make you aware of how python works, and the general philosophy behind python programming. If some of the concepts that are introduced here seem abstract or overly complex, just try to get a general feel for the idea, and the details will be fleshed out later

1.4.1 Basic Core Language

Python is designed so that there really isn't that much to learn in the basic language. For example, there is only one basic structure for conditional pro-gramming (if/else/elif), two looping commands (while and for), and a consistent method of handling errors (try/except) which apply to all python programs. This doesn't mean that the language is not flexible and powerful, however. It simply means that you're not confronted with an overwhelming choice of options at every turn, which can make programming a much simpler task.

CHAPTER 1.

INTRODUCTION

1.4.2 Modules

Python relies on modules, that is, self-contained programs which define a variety of functions and data types, that you can call in order to do tasks be-yond the scope of the basic core language by using the import command. For example, the core distribution of python contains modules for processing files, accessing your computer's operating system and the internet, writing CGI scripts (which handle communicating with pages displayed in web browsers), string handling and many other tasks. Optional modules, available on the Python web site (http://www.python.org), can be used to create graphical user interfaces, communicate with data bases, process image files, and so on. This structure makes it easy to get started with python, learning specific skills only as you need them, as well as making python run more efficiently by not always including every capability in every program.

1.4.3 Object Oriented Programming

Python is a true object-oriented language. The term "object oriented" has become quite a popular buzzword; such high profile languages as C++ and Java are both object oriented by design. Many other languages add some object-oriented capabilities, but were not designed to be object oriented from the ground up as python was. Why is this feature important? Object ori-ented program allows you to focus on the data you're interested in, whether it's employee information, the results of a scientific experiment or survey, setlists for your favorite band, the contents of your CD collection, informa-tion entered by an internet user into a search form or shopping cart, and to develop methods to deal efficiently with your data. A basic concept of object oriented programming is encapsulation, the ability to define an object that contains your data and all the information a program needs to operate on that data. In this way, when you call a function (known as a method in object-oriented lingo), you don't need to specify a lot of details about your data, because your data object "knows" all about itself. In addition, objects can inherit from other objects, so if you or someone else has designed an ob-ject that's very close to one you're interested in, you only have to construct those methods which differ from the existing object, allowing you to save a lot of work.

Another nice feature of object oriented programs is operator overloading. What this means is that the same operator can have different meanings

1.4. BASIC PRINCIPLES OF PYTHON

13

when used with different types of data. For example, in python, when you're dealing with numbers, the plus sign (+) has its usual obvious meaning of addition. But when you're dealing with strings, the plus sign means to join the two strings together. In addition to being able to use overloading for built-in types (like numbers and strings), python also allows you to define what operators mean for the data types you create yourself.

Perhaps the nicest feature of object-oriented programming in python is that you can use as much or as little of it as you want. Until you get comfortable with the ideas behind object-oriented programming, you can write more traditional programs in python without any problems.

1.4.4 Namespaces and Variable Scoping

When you type the name of a variable inside a script or interactive python session, python needs to figure out exactly what variable you're using. To prevent variables you create from overwriting or interfering with variables in python itself or in the modules you use, python uses the concept of multiple namespaces. Basically, this means that the same variable name can be used in different parts of a program without fear of destroying the value of a variable you're not concerned with.

To keep its bookkeeping in order, python enforces what is known as the LGB rule. First, the local namespace is searched, then the global names-pace, then the namespace of python built-in functions and variables. A local namespace is automatically created whenever you write a function, or a module containing any of functions, class definitions, or methods. The global namespace consists primarily of the variables you create as part of the "top-level" program, like a script or an interactive session. Finally, the built-in namespace consists of the objects which are part of python's core. You can see the contents of any of the namespaces by using the dir command:

>>> dir()

['__builtins__', '__doc__', '__name__']

>>> dir(__builtins__)

['ArithmeticError', 'AssertionError', 'AttributeError', 'EOFError', 'Ellipsis', 'Exception', 'FloatingPointError', 'IOError', 'ImportError', 'IndexError', 'KeyError', 'KeyboardInterrupt', 'LookupError', 'MemoryError', 'NameError', 'None', 'OverflowError', 'RuntimeError', 'StandardError', 'SyntaxError', 'SystemError', 'SystemExit', 'TypeError', 'ValueError', 'ZeroDivisionError', '_', '__debug__', '__doc__',

CHAPTER 1. INTRODUCTION

'__import__', '__name__', 'abs', 'apply', 'callable', 'chr', 'cmp', 'coerce', 'compile', 'complex', 'delattr', 'dir', 'divmod', 'eval', 'execfile', 'filter', 'float', 'getattr', 'globals', 'hasattr', 'hash', 'hex', 'id', 'input', 'int', 'intern', 'isinstance', 'issubclass', 'len', 'list', 'locals', 'long', 'map', 'max', 'min', 'oct', 'open', 'ord', 'pow', 'range', 'raw_input', 'reduce', 'reload', 'repr', 'round', 'setattr', 'slice', 'str', 'tuple', 'type', 'vars', 'xrange']

The __builtins__ namespace contains all the functions, variables and ex-ceptions which are part of python's core.

To give controlled access to other namespaces, python uses the import statement. There are three ways to use this statement. In its simplest form, you import the name of a module; this allows you to specify the various objects defined in that module by using a two level name, with the mod-ule's name and the object's name separated by a period. For example, the string module (Section 8.4) provides many functions useful for dealing with character strings. Suppose we want to use the split function of the string module to break up a sentence into a list containing separate words. We could use the following sequence of statements:

ft. import string

ft. string.split('Welcome to the Ministry of Silly Walks') ['Welcome', 'to', 'the', 'Ministry', 'of', 'Silly', 'Walks']

If we had tried to refer to this function as simply "split", python would not be able to find it. That's because we have only imported the string module into the local namespace, not all of the objects defined in the module. (See below for details of how to do that.)

The second form of the import statement is more specific; it specifies the individual objects from a module whose names we want imported into the local namespace. For example, if we only needed the two functions split and join for use in a program, we could import just those two names directly into the local namespace, allowing us to dispense with the string. prefix:

ft. from string import split,join

ft. split('Welcome to the Ministry of Silly Walks') ['Welcome', 'to', 'the', 'Ministry', 'of', 'Silly', 'Walks']

This technique reduces the amount of typing we need to do, and is an efficient way to bring just a few outside objects into the local environment.

Finally, some modules are designed so that you're expected to have top-level access to all of the functions in the module without having to use the module name as a prefix. In cases like this you can use a statement like:

```
>>> from string import *
```

Now all of the objects defined in the string module are available directly in the top-level environment, with no need for a prefix. You should use this technique with caution, because certain commonly used names from the module may override the names of your variables. In addition, it introduces lots of names into the local namespace, which could adversely affect python's efficiency.

1.4.5 Exception Handling

Regardless how carefully you write your programs, when you start using them in a variety of situations, errors are bound to occur. Python provides a consistent method of handling errors, a topic often refered to as exception handling. When you're performing an operation that might result in an error, you can surround it with a try loop, and provide an except clause to tell python what to do when a particular error arises. While this is a fairly advanced concept, usually found in more complex languages, you can start using it in even your earliest python programs.

As a simple example, consider dividing two numbers. If the divisor is zero, most programs (python included) will stop running, leaving the user back at a system shell prompt, or with nothing at all. Here's a little python program that illustrates this concept; assume we've saved it to a file called div.py:

```
#!/usr/local/bin/python
x = 7
y = 0
print x/y
print "Now we're done!"
```

When we run this program, we don't get to the line which prints the message, because the division by zero is a “fatal” error:

```
% div.py
Traceback (innermost last):
```



```
File "div.py", line 5, in ?
print x/y
ZeroDivisionError: integer division or modulo
```

While the message may look a little complicated, the main point to notice is that the last line of the message tells us the name of the exception that occured. This allows us to construct an except clause to handle the problem:

```
x = 7
y = 0
try:
print x/y
except ZeroDivisionError:
print "Oops - I can't divide by zero, sorry!"
print "Now we're done!"
```

Now when we run the program, it behaves a little more nicely:

```
% div.py
```

Oops - I can't divide by zero, sorry!

Now we're done!

Since each exception in python has a name, it's very easy to modify your program to handle errors whenever they're discovered. And of course, if you can think ahead, you can construct try/except clauses to catch errors before they happen.

Chapter 2

String Data

2.1 String Constants

Strings are a collection of characters which are stored together to represent arbitrary text inside a python program. You can create a string constant inside a python program by surrounding text with either single quotes ('), double quotes ("), or a collection of three of either types of quotes (''' or

"""). In the first two cases, the opening and closing quotes must appear on the same line in your program; when you use triple quotes, your text can span as many lines as you like. The choice of which quote symbol to use is up to you – both single and double quotes have the same meaning in python.

Here are a few examples of how to create a string constant and assign its value to a variable:

name = 'Phil'

value = "$7.00"

helptext = """You can create long strings of text spanning several lines by using triple quotes at the beginning and end of the text"""

When the variable helptext is printed (using the print command; Sec-tion 5.1), it would display as three lines, with the line breaks at the same points as in the triple-quoted text.

You can also create strings by reading input from a file (Section 5.4.1), or by concatenating smaller strings (Section 2.4.1).

17

18

CHAPTER 2. STRING DATA

Sequence

Meaning

Sequence

Meaning

\

continuation

\\

literal backslash

\'

single quote

\"

double quote

\a

bell

\b

backspace

\e

escape character

\0

null terminator

\n

newline

\t
horizontal tab
\f
form feed
\r
carriage return
\0XX
octal character XX
\xXX
hexadecimal value XX
Table 2.1: Special Characters in Strings

2.2 Special Characters and Raw Strings

Inside of any of the pairs of quotes described in the previous section, there are special character sequences, beginning with a backslash (\), which are interpreted in a special way. Table 2.1 lists these characters.

Using a single backslash as a continuation character is an alternative to using triple quoted strings when you are constructing a string constant. Thus, the following two expressions are equivalent, but most programmers prefer the convenience of not having to use backslashes which is offered by triple quotes.

threelines = 'First\
Second\
Third'
threelines = '''First
Second
Third'''

The backslashed quote symbols are useful if you need to create a string with both single and double quotes. (If you have only one kind of quotes in your string, you can simply use the other kind to surround your string, since the two types of quotes are equivalent in python.)

As Table 2.1 shows, you can produce a backslash in a string by typing two backslashes; note that only one of the backslashes will actually appear in the string when it's printed. There are certain situations (most notably when constructing regular expressions (Section 8.5)), when typing two back-slashes to get a single backslash becomes tedious. Python provides what are

2.3. UNICODE STRINGS

19

called raw strings, in which the character sequences shown in Table 2.1 have no special meaning. To construct a raw string, precede the opening quote character with either a lowercase or uppercase "R" (r or R). Note, however that a backslash cannot be the very last character of a raw string. Thus, these two expressions are equivalent:

ft. print 'Here is a backslash: \\ ' Here is a backslash: \

ft. print r'Here is a backslash: \ ' Here is a backslash: \

2.3 Unicode Strings

Starting with version 2.0, python provides support for Unicode strings, whose characters are stored in 16 bits instead of the 8 bits used by a normal string. To specify that a string should be stored using this format, precede the open-ing quote character with either a lowercase or uppercase "U". In addition, an arbitrary Unicode character can be specified with the notation "\uhhhh", where hhhh represents a four-digit hexadecimal number.

Notice that if a unicode string is combined with a regular string, the resulting string will also be a Unicode string.

2.4 String Operations

The following subsections describe some of the operations that are available with strings.

2.4.1 Concatenation

The addition operator (+) takes on the role of concatenation when used with strings, that is, the result of "adding" two strings together is a new string which consists of the original strings put together:

ft. first = 'black'

ft. second = 'jack'

ft. first + second 'blackjack'

20 CHAPTER 2. STRING DATA

No space or other character is inserted between concatenated strings. If you do want a space, you can simply add it:

ft. first + " " + second 'black jack'

When the strings you want to concatenate are literal string constants, that is, pieces of text surrounded by any of the quotes that python accepts, you don't even need the plus sign; python will automatically concatenate string constants that are separated by whitespace:

ft. nums = "one " "two " "three "

ft. nums

'one two three '

You can freely mix variables and string constants together — anywhere that python expects a string, it can be either a variable or a constant:

ft. msg = """Send me email

... My address is """

ft. msg + "me@myplace.com"

'Send me email\012My address is me@myplace.com'

Notice that the newline which was entered in the triple quoted string appears as \012, the octal representation of the (non-printable) newline character. When you use the print command, the newline is displayed as you would expect:

ft. print msg + 'me@myplace.com' Send me email

My address is me@myplace.com

Remember that python considers the type of an object when it tries to apply an operator, so that if you try to concatenate a string and a number, you'll have problems:

ft. x = 12./7.

ft. print 'The answer is ' + x Traceback (innermost last):

File "<stdin>", line 1, in ?

TypeError: illegal argument type for built-in operation

2.4. STRING OPERATIONS

21

The number (x) must first be converted to a string before it can be con-catentated. Python provides two ways to do this: the core function repr, or the backquote operator (“). The following example shows both of these techniques used to solve the problem of concatenating strings and numbers:

ft. print 'The answer is ' + repr(x) The answer is 1.71428571429

ft. print 'The answer is ' + ‘x‘

The answer is 1.71428571429

Notice that python uses its default of 12 significant figures; if you want more control over the way numbers are converted to strings, see Section 5.2, where the percent operator (%) for string formatting is introduced.

When you want to concatenate lots of strings together, the join method for strings (Section 2.4.4), or the join function in the string module (Sec-tion 8.4.2) are more convenient.

2.4.2 Repetition

The asterisk (*), when used between a string and an integer creates a new string with the old string repeated by the value of the integer. The order of the arguments is not important. So the following two statements will both print ten dashes:

ft. '-' * 10 '----------'

ft. 10 * '-' '----------'

Trying to use the repetition operator between two strings results in a Type Error exception.

2.4.3 Indexing and Slicing

Strings in python support indexing and slicing. To extract a single character from a string, follow the string with the index of the desired character sur-rounded by square brackets ([ ]), remembering that the first character of a string has index zero.

22 CHAPTER 2. STRING DATA

ft. what = 'This parrot is dead'

ft. what[3]

's'

ft. what[0]

'T'

If the subscript you provide between the brackets is less than zero, python counts from the end of the string, with a subscript of -1 representing the last character in the string.

ft. what[-1]

'd'

To extract a contiguous piece of a string (known as a slice), use a subscript consisting of the starting position followed by a colon (:), finally followed by one more than the ending position of the slice you want to extract. Notice that the slicing stops immediately before the second value:

ft. what[0:4]

'This'

ft. what[5:11]

'parrot'

One way to think about the indexes in a slice is that you give the starting position as the value before the colon, and the starting position plus the number of characters in the slice after the colon.

For the special case when a slice starts at the beginning of a string, or continues until the end, you can omit the first or second index, respectively. So to extract all but the first character of a string, you can use a subscript of 1: .

>>> what[1:]

'his parrot is dead'

To extract the first 3 characters of a string you can use :3 .

ft. what[:3]

'Thi'

If you use a value for a slice index which is larger than the length of the string, python does not raise an exceptrion, but treats the index as if it was the length of the string.

As always, variables and integer constants can be freely mixed:

ft. start = 3

ft. finish = 8

ft. what[start:finish] 's par'

ft. what[5:finish]

'par'

Using a second index which is less than or equal to the first index will result in an empty string. If either index is not an integer, a TypeError exception is raised unless, of course, that index was omitted.

2.4.4 Functions and Methods for Character Strings

The core language provides only one function which is useful for working with strings; the len function, which returns the number of characters which a character string contains. In versions of Python earlier than 2.0, tools for working with strings were provided by the string module (Section 8.4). Starting with version 2.0, strings in python became "true" objects, and a variety of methods were introduced to operate on strings. If you find that the string methods described in this section are not available with your version of python, refer to Section 8.4 for equivalent capabilities through the string module. (Note that on some systems, a newer version of Python may be available through the name python2.)

Since strings are the first true objects we've encountered a brief descrip-tion of methods is in order. As mentioned earlier (Section 1.4.3), when dealing with objects, functions are known as methods. Besides the terminol-ogy, methods are invoked slightly differently than functions. When you call a function like len, you pass the arguments in a comma separated list sur-rounded by parentheses after the function name. When you invoke a method, you provide the name of the object the method is to act upon, followed by a period, finally followed by the method name and the parenthesized list of ad-ditional arguments. Remember to provide empty parentheses if the method does not take any arguments, so that python can distinguish a method call with no arguments from a reference to a variable stored within the object.

Strings in python are immutable objects; this means that you can't change the value of a string in place. If you do want to change the value of a string, you need to invoke a method on the variable containing the string you wish to change, and to reassign the value of that operation to the variable in

24 CHAPTER 2. STRING DATA

question, as some of the examples below will show.

Many of the string methods provided by python are listed in Table 2.2. Among the most useful are the methods split and join. The split method operates on a string, and returns a list, each of whose elements is a word in the original string, where a word is defined by default as a group of non-whitespace characters, joined by one or more whitespace characters. If you provide one optional argument to the split method, it is used to split the string as an alternative to one or more whitespace characters. Note the sub-tle difference between invoking split with no arguments, and an argument consisting of a single blank space:

ft. str = 'This parrot is dead'

ft. str.split()

['This', 'parrot', 'is', 'dead']
>>> str.split(' ')
['This', 'parrot', '', 'is', 'dead']

When more than one space is encountered in the string, the default method treats it as if it were just a single space, but when we explicitly set the separator character to a single space, multiple spaces in the string result in extra elements in the resultant list. You can also obtain the default behavior for split by specifying None for the sep argument.

The maxsplit argument to the split method will result in a list with maxsplit + 1 elements. This can be very useful when you only need to split part of a string, since the remaining pieces will be put into a single element of the list which is returned. For example, suppose you had a file containing definitions of words, with the word being the first string and the definition consisting of the remainder of the line. By setting maxsplit to 1, the word would become the first element of the returned list, and the definition would become the second element of the list, as the following example shows:

ft. line = 'Ni a sound that a knight makes'

ft. line.split(maxsplit=1)

['Ni', 'a sound that a knight makes']

In some versions of python, the split method will not accept a named argument for maxsplit. In that case, you would need to explicitly specify the separator, using None to obtain the default behavior.

>>> line.split(None,1)
['Ni', 'a sound that a knight makes']

2.4. STRING OPERATIONS

Split and Join

Name
Purpose
Arguments
join
Insert a string between each element of a sequence
sequence
split
Create a list from “words” in a string
sep(optional)
maxsplit(optional)
splitlines
Create a list from lines in a string
keepends(optional)

Methods for searching
Note: Each of these functions accepts optional arguments start and end which limit the range of the search.
Name
Purpose
Arguments
count
Count the number of occurences of substring
substring
find
Return the lowest index where substring is found,
substring
and -1 if not found
index
Like find, but raises ValueError if not found
substring
rfind
Return the highest index where substring is found,
substring
and -1 if not found
rindex
Like rfind, but raises ValueError if not found
substring
Methods for Justification
Name
Purpose
Arguments
center
Centers a string in a given width
width
ljust
Left justifies a string
width
lstrip
Removes leading whitespace
rjust
Right justifies a string
width
rstrip
Removes trailing whitespace
strip
Removes leading and trailing whitespace
Methods for Case (upper/lower)
Name
Purpose
Arguments
capitalize
Capitalize the first letter of the string
lower

Make all characters lower case
swapcase
Change upper to lower and lower to upper
title
Capitalize the first letter of each word in the string
upper
Make all characters upper case
Table 2.2: String Methods
26 CHAPTER 2. STRING DATA

When using the join method for strings, remember that the method operates on the string which will be used between each element of the joined list, not on the list itself. This may result in some unusual looking statements:

ft. words = ['spam','spam','bacon','spam']

ft. ' '.join(words)

'spam spam bacon spam'

Of course, you could assign the value of ' ' to a variable to improve the appearance of such a statement.

The index and find functions can be useful when trying to extract sub-strings, although techniques using the re module (Section 8.5) will generally be more powerful. As an example of the use of these functions, suppose we have a string with a parenthesized substring, and we wish to extract just that substring. Using the slicing techniques explained in Section 2.4.3, and locating the substring using, for example index and rindex, here's one way to solve the problem:

ft. model = 'Turbo Accelerated Widget (MMX-42b) Press'

ft. try:

... model[model.index('(') + 1 : model.rindex(')')]
... except ValueError:
... print 'No parentheses found'
...
'MMX-42b'

When you use these functions, make sure to check for the case where the substring is not found, either the ValueError raised by the index functions, or the returned value of -1 from the find functions.

Remember that the string methods will not change the value of the string they are acting on, but you can achieve the same effect by overwriting the string with the returned value of the method. For example, to replace a string with an equivalent version consisting of all upper-case characters, statements like the following could be used:

ft. language = 'python'

ft. language = language.upper()

ft. language

'PYTHON'
2.4. STRING OPERATIONS

27

Finally, python offers a variety of so-called predicate methods, which take no arguments, and return 1 if all the characters in a string are of a particular type, and 0 otherwise. These functions, whose use should be obvious from their names, include isalnum, isalpha, isdigit, islower, isspace, istitle, and isupper.

Related modules: string, re, stringIO.

Related exceptions: TypeError, IndexError.

28

Chapter 3-Numeric Data

3.1 Types of Numeric Data

Python supports four types of numeric objects: integers, long integers, float-ing point numbers, and complex numbers. In general, python will not au-tomatically convert numbers from one type to another, although it provides a complete set of functions to allow you to explicitly do these conversions (Section 3.2).

To enter numeric data inside an interactive python session or in a script, simply set the value of a variable to the desired number. To specify a floating point number, either include a decimal point somewhere in the number, or use exponential notation, for example 1e3 or 1E3 to represent 1000 (1 times 10 to the third power). Note that when using exponentional notation, numbers are always stored as floating point, even if there is no decimal point.

Long integers can be entered by following an ordinary integer with the letter "L", either lowercase (e.g. 27l) or uppercase (e.g. 27L). (Since a lowercase "l" looks so much like the number "1", you may want to get in the habit of using uppercase "L"s in this context.) In python, long integers are actually what are sometimes called "arbitrary precision" integers, since they can have as many digits as you have the patience to type into the computer. On most computers, ordinary integers have a range from about -2 billion to +2 billion. Trying to use an integer larger than this value results in an OverlowError:

ft. x = 2000000000

ft. x = x + x / 2

CHAPTER 3. NUMERIC DATA

Traceback (innermost last):

File "<stdin>", line 1, in ?

OverflowError: integer addition

You'll never see such an error when using a long integer:

ft. x = 2000000000L

ft. x = x + x / 2

ft. x

3000000000L

A further advantage of long integers is that all arithemetic performed with long integers will be exact, unlike floating point numbers which have a limited precision (about 15 or 16 digits on most computers). It comes as a surprise to many people that adding a small floating point number to a very large floating point number will not change the original floating point number. (In the following example, I'll use some formatted I/O features explained more fully in Section 5.2):

ft. x = 1e16

ft. '%f' % x '10000000000000000.000000'

ft. x1 = x + 1.

ft. '%f' % x1 '10000000000000000.000000'

The addition of 1 to such a huge number makes no difference because of the limited precision of floating point numbers. However, all integer arithmetic is exact when using long integers:

ft. xl = long(x)

ft. xl 10000000000000000L

ft. xl + 1 10000000000000001L

(As explained in Section 3.2, the long function converts its argument into a long integer.) While it might be tempting to store all integers as long inte-gers, remember that, while regular integer arithmetic is supported by most operating systems, python has to perform all its own long integer arithmetic,

3.1. TYPES OF NUMERIC DATA

31

so using long integers will definitely slow your programs down. But if you know your numbers will fall outside the range of a normal integer, long inte-gers can be a very useful tool.

Complex numbers can be entered into python using either the complex function, or by denoting the complex number as the real portion followed by a plus sign, followed by the imaginary portion with a trailing "J" (ei-ther upper or lower case). There can be no spaces between the imaginary portion and the "J". Thus 3.2 + 7j is a valid complex number, but 3.2

- 7 j is not. The complex function can be called with either one or two arguments representing the real component or the real and imaginary com-ponents respectively; complex(3.2,7) is equivalent to the previous example. Regardless of how you enter a complex number, both components are stored as floating point numbers.

3.1.1 Hexadecimal and Octal Constants

As an alternative to decimal constants, python allows you to enter numbers as either octal (base 8) or hexadecimal (base 16) constants. Octal constants are recognized by python because they start with a leading zero (0); in particular a number like 012 is interpreted as an octal number (with a decimal value of 10), not as a decimal number with a leading zero, and a number like 09 will generate a SyntaxError exception, since 9 is not a valid octal digit.

Hexadecimal constants start with a leading zero, followed by the letter "x" (either upper or lower case). In addition to the decimal digits, these constants can contain the letters a, b, c, d, e, or f (again, either upper or lower case), representing the extra hexadecimal digits beyond 9.

Note that these constants are numeric values, not string values, and thus should not be surrounded by quotes. Trying to use a string representation of an octal or hexadecimal constants raises a TypeError exception.

Arithmetic performed on octal or hexadecimal numbers will be displayed in decimal form by the python interpreter. The functions hex and oct convert their arguments into a string representation of the corresponding hexadecimal or octal value, respectively.

3.1.2 Numeric Operators

Python supports the full set of binary arithmetic operators that you would expect in a modern computer language. A binary operator is one which per-

CHAPTER 3. NUMERIC DATA

Operator

Function

Operator	Function
+	Addition
-	Subtraction
*	Multiplication
/	Division
>>	Right bit shift
<<	Left bit shift
**	Exponentiation
%	Modulus

Table 3.1: Arithmetic Operators

forms an operation on exactly two elements, one on each side of the operator's symbol. Table 3.1 shows the operators supported by python.

When performing operations on integers, be aware that python performs integer arithmetic unless at least one of the operands is a floating point number. See Section 3.2 for further information.

In addition to the binary operators in Table 3.1, python also provides unary operators for plus and minus. Thus any number or expression which returns a single numeric value can be preceded by either a minus sign (-) or a plus sign (+).

3.1.3 Functions for Numeric Data

A few basic mathematical functions are part of python's core; many more can be found in the math module.

The abs function returns the absolute value of its argument, that is, the value itself if it is greater than or equal to 0, and the negative of the value otherwise. The round function performs rounding on its argument. Unlike integer arithmetic, which simply drops any fractional portion of a number, round returns a floating point representation of the nearest integer of its argument, truncating when the fraction is less than 0.5, and advancing to the next integer when the fraction is greater than 0.5.

The divmod function accepts two numeric arguments, and returns a tuple (Section 4.5) containing two floating point values. The first argument is divided by the second argument, and the function returns (in the first element of the tuple) the number of times the second element goes into the first and (in the second element of the tuple) the remainder. The divmod function accepts either integer or floating point arguments:

ft. divmod(21,4) (5, 1)

ft. divmod(25.8,.7)

(36.0, 0.6)

Note that, in the first example, 21 = 5 * 4 + 1, and in the second exam-ple 25.8 = 36 * 0.7 + 0.6. The modulus function found in many other languages returns the second element of the tuple returned by divmod.

The pow function is an alternative to the exponentiation operator (**). It accepts two arguments; the first is the numerical expression to be raised to a power, and the second is the power to which the number should be raised. Provided with two integer arguments, pow returns an integer; if either of the arguments is a floating point number, it will return a floating point number. Similarly, if a long integer is provided as the first argument, it will return a long integer, unless the second argument is a floating point number.

Related modules: array, cmath, math, random

Related exceptions: ZeroDivisionError, OverflowError, FloatingPointError

3.2 Conversion of Scalar Types

In general, python will not automatically convert objects from one type to another, but instead provides functions to allow these conversions to be per-formed. One area which requires particular caution is integer arithmetic. When python evaluates arithmetic expressions which contain only integers, it performs its operations using integer arithmetic. For addition subtrac-tion, and multiplication, this will not result in any surprises, but for division python truncates its results to the nearest integer smaller than the answer. If at least one of the numbers involved in the expression containing the division is a floating point number, then the integers involved in the computation will be temporarily converted to floating point numbers for the purpose of the computation only. The following example illustrates some of these points, as well as introducing the float conversion function.

ft. x = 3

ft. y = 2

ft. x / y

1

ft. float(x) / y

1.5

ft. float(x/y)

34 CHAPTER 3. NUMERIC DATA

1.0

Since the values of the variables x and y were entered as integers, any arith-metic operations involving them will be carried out using integer arithmetic; thus, when 3 is divided by 2, the (integer) answer is 1. By converting either operand to a float, the expected result of 1.5 can be obtained. Other numeric conversion routines include long and int.

When values in a computation are numbers rather than variable names, it suffices to include a decimal point in any of the operands of an arithmetic expression to insure that the entire computation will be carried out using floating point arithmetic, but there is no harm in including decimal points (or exponential notation) for all the operands. Thus the following expressions all result in the same answer:

ft. 3./2

1.5

ft. 3/2.

1.5

ft. 3./2.

1.5

These conversion routines are also necessary to convert numbers repre-sented as strings into actual python numeric values. If you attempt to use a string value, even if it is a representaion of a number, as a numeric value, it will raise a TypeError:

>>> '3' / 2.

Traceback (innermost last):

File "<stdin>", line 1, in ?

TypeError: bad operand type(s) for /

Simply pass the string to the appropriate conversion function (float, int or long) to fix the error:

ft. float('3') / 2.

1.5

This same technique is required when numbers are read from a file, since in this case they will enter the python environment as strings.

If you have two numeric values and simply want to convert them to a common type, the function coerce can be used. If you consider the hierarchy

3.2. CONVERSION OF SCALAR TYPES

35

of integer, long integer, floating point number and complex number, coerce converts the argument which is lower in the hierarchy to the type of the argument which is higher. The following examples illustrate this point:

ft. coerce(3,5L) (3L, 5L)

ft. coerce(3,5.) (3.0, 5.0)

ft. coerce(3L,5.) (3.0, 5.0)

ft. coerce(3.,2.+1j) ((3+0j), (2+1j))

One other area where explicit conversion is needed is when trying to operate on numbers and strings together. Since python relies on operator overloading to perform many common tasks, it will generate a TypeError when you ask it to perform such operations on dissimilar types. For example, consider the variable a, with a numeric value of 7, and the variable b with the string value of “8”. What should python do when you ask to “add” together these two values?

ft. a = 7

ft. b = '8'

ft. a + b

Traceback (innermost last):

File "<stdin>", line 1, in ?

TypeError: number coercion failed

Since the answer isn't clear, python raises the exception. There are two possibilities: treat a as a string, and concatenate it with b, or treat b as a number and add it to a. The builtin function str can be used to temporarily convert a number to its string representation; any of the conversion functions mentioned in the previous paragraphs can be used to convert a string to a number.

ft. str(a) + b '78'

ft. a + int(b)

15

36 CHAPTER 3. NUMERIC DATA

Python will always be able to convert numbers to strings, but it will raise a ValueError exception if you attempt to convert a string to a number when that string does not represent a number.

Chapter 4

Lists, Tuples and Dictionaries

4.1 List Data

Lists provide a general mechanism for storing a collection of objects indexed by a number in python. The elements of the list are arbitrary — they can be numbers, strings, functions, user-defined objects or even other lists, making complex data structures very simple to express in python. You can input a list to the python interpreter by surrounding a comma separated list of the objects you want in the list with square brackets ([ ]) Thus, a simple list of numbers can be created as follows:

>>> mylist = [1,7,9, 13, 22, 31]

Python ignores spaces between the entries of a list. If you need to span multiple lines with a list entry, you can simply hit the return key after any comma in the list:

ft. newlist = [7, 9, 12, 15,

... 17,19,103]

Note that the python interpreter changes its prompt when it recognizes a continuation line, and that no indentation is necessary to continue a line like this. Inside a script, your input can also be broken up after commas in a similar fashion. To create an empty list, use square brackets with no elements in between them ([]).

The elements of a list need not be of the same type. The following list contains numeric, string and list data, along with a function:

CHAPTER 4. LISTS, TUPLES AND DICTIONARIES

>>> mixlist = [7,'dog','tree',[1,5,2,7],abs]

Since the token abs was entered in the list without quotes, python interprets it as a named object; in this case it represents the builtin function abs. Since functions and many other objects can't be displayed in the same fashion as a number or a string, python uses a special notation to display them:

>>> mixlist

[7, 'dog', 'tree', [1, 5, 2, 7], <built-in function abs>]

The angle brackets surrounding the phrase "built-in function abs" indicate that that element of the list is a special object of some sort.

To access the individual elements of a list, use square brackets after the list's name surrounding the index of the desired element. Recall that the first element of a sequence in python is numbered zero. Thus, to extract the abs function from mylist in the example above, we would refer to element 4, i.e. mylist[4]:

ft. mixlist[4](-5)

5

This example shows that once an element is extracted from a list, you can use it in any context in which the original element could be used; by providing an argument in parentheses to mixlist[4], we call the function abs which was stored in that position in the list. Furthermore, when accessing lists inside of lists, you can simply use additional sets of square brackets to access individual elements:

ft. nestlist = [1,2,[10,20,30,[7,9,11,[100,200,300]]],[1,7,8]]

ft. nestlist[2]

[10, 20, 30, [7, 9, 11, [100, 200, 300]]]
>>> nestlist[2][3]
[7, 9, 11, [100, 200, 300]]

ft. nestlist[2][3][3] [100, 200, 300]

ft. nestlist[2][3][3][0]

100

While this is a competely artificial example, it shows that you can nest lists to any level you choose, and that the individual elements of those lists are always extracted in a simple, consistent way.

4.2. LIST INDEXING AND SLICING

39

You may notice a similarity between the way you access elements in a list, and the way you access individual characters in a character string (Sec-tion 2.4.3). This is because both strings and lists are examples of python sequences, and they behave consistently. For example, to find out the num-ber of elements in a list, you can use the built-in function len, just as you would to find the number of characters in a character string. Calling len with a non-sequence argument results in a TypeError exception, however.

ft. len(mixlist)

5

ft. len(mixlist[3])

4

ft. len(mixlist[1])

3

ft. len(mixlist[0]) Traceback (innermost last):

File "<stdin>", line 1, in ? TypeError: len() of unsized object

In the first case, calling len with the argument mixlist returns the number of elements in the list, namely 5. Similarly, refering to mixlist[3], corre-sponding to the list [1, 5, 2, 7] returns 4, the number of elements in that list. Calling len with mixlist[1] (which is the string “dog”) returns the number of characters in the string, but calling len with the scalar argument mixlist[0] (which is the integer 7), results in an exception.

To convert a string into a list, making each character in the string a separate element in the resulting list, use the list function.

4.2 List Indexing and Slicing

The slicing operations introduced in Section 2.4.3 also work with lists, with one very useful addition. As well as using slicing to extract part of a list (i.e. a slice on the right hand sign of an equal sign), you can set the value of elements in a list by using a slice on the left hand side of an equal sign. In python terminology, this is because lists are mutable objects, while strings are immutable. Simply put, this means that once a string's value is established, it can't be changed without creating a new variable, while a list can be modified (lengthened, shortened, rearranged, etc.) without having to store

40 CHAPTER 4. LISTS, TUPLES AND DICTIONARIES

the results in a new variable, or reassign the value of an expression to the original variable name.

Consider a list with 5 integer elements:

>>> thelist = [0,5,10,15,20]

Now suppose we wish to change the central three elements (5, 10 and 15, at positions 1, 2 and 3 in the list) to the values 6, 7, and 8. As with a string, we could extract the three elements with a statement like:

ft. thelist[1:4] [5, 10, 15]

But with a list, we can also assign values to that slice:

ft. thelist[1:4] = [6,7,8]

ft. thelist

[0, 6, 7, 8, 20]

If the number of elements in the list on the right hand side of the equal sign is not equal to the number of elements implied by the subscript of the slice, the list will expand or shrink to accomodate the assignment. (Recall that the number of elements in a slice is the higher valued subscript minus the lower valued subscript.) The following examples illustrate this point:

ft. words = ['We','belong','to','the','knights','who','say','"Ni"']

ft. words[1:4] = ['are']

ft. words

['We', 'are', 'knights', 'who', 'say', '"Ni"']

>>> words[1:2] = ['are','a','band','of']

['We', 'are', 'a', 'band', 'of', 'knights', 'who', 'say', '"Ni"']

Note that when we are replacing a slice with a single element, it must be surrounded by square brackets, effectively making it into a list with one element, to avoid a TypeError exception.

Assignments through slicing differ from those done with simple subscript-ing in that a slice can change the length of a list, while assignments done through a single subscript will always preserve the length of the list. This is true for slices where both of the subscripts are the same. Notice the difference between the two expressions shown below:

4.2. LIST INDEXING AND SLICING

41

ft. # using a single subscript

ft. x = ['one','two','three','four','five']

ft. x[1] = ['dos','tres','cuatro']

ft. x

['one', ['dos', 'tres', 'cuatro'], 'three', 'four', 'five']

ft. # using a slice

ft. x = ['one','two','three','four','five']

ft. x[1:1] = ['dos','tres','cuatro']

ft. x

ft. ['one', 'dos', 'tres', 'cuatro', 'two', 'three', 'four', 'five']

In the final example, we were able to insert three elements into an list without replacing any elements in the list by assigning to a slice where both subscripts were the same.

Another use of slices is to make a separate modifiable copy of a list. (See Section 6.1 to understand why this is important.) In this case, you create a slice without either a starting or ending index. Python will then make a complete copy of the list

ft. x = ['one','two','three']

ft. y = x[:]

ft. y

['one', 'two', 'three']

One final use of slices is to remove elements from an array. If we try to replace a single element or slice of an array with an empty list, that empty list will literally replace the locations to which it's assigned. But if we replace a slice of an array with an empty list, that slice of the array is effectively removed:

ft. a = [1,3,5,7,9]

ft. a[2] = []

ft. a

[1, 3, [], 7, 9]

ft. b = [2,4,6,8]

ft. b[2:3] = []

ft. b

[2, 4, 8]

42 CHAPTER 4. LISTS, TUPLES AND DICTIONARIES

Another way to remove items from a list is to use the del statement. You provide the del statement with the element or slice of a list which you want removed, and that element or slice is removed without a trace. So to remove the second element from the list a in the previous example, we would use the del statement as follows:

ft. del a[2]

ft. a

[1, 3, 7, 9]

The del statement is just as effective with slices:

ft. nums = ['one','two','three','four','five']

ft. del nums[0:3]

ft. nums

['four', 'five']

In the previous example, the same result could be obtained by assigning an empty list to nums[0:3].

4.3 List Operators

A number of operators are overloaded with respect to lists, making some common operations very simple to express.

4.3.1 Concatenation

To combine the contents of two lists, use a plus sign (+) between the two lists to be concatenated. The result is a single list whose length is the total of the length of the two lists being combined, and which contains all of the elements of the first list followed by all of the elements of the second list.

ft. first = [7,9,'dog']

ft. second = ['cat',13,14,12]

ft. first + second

[7, 9, 'dog', 'cat', 13, 14, 12]

Alternatively, you can combine two lists with the expand method (Sec-tion 4.4).

4.3. LIST OPERATORS

43

Note that list concatenation only works when you're combining two lists. To add a scalar to the end of a list, you can either surround the scalar with square brackets ([ ]), or invoke the append method (Section 4.4).

4.3.2 Repetition

Like strings, the asterisk (*) is overloaded for lists to serve as a repetition operator. The result of applying repetition to a list is a single list, with the elements of the original list repeated as many times as you specify:

>>> ['a','b','c'] * 4

['a', 'b', 'c', 'a', 'b', 'c', 'a', 'b', 'c', 'a', 'b', 'c']

Special care needs to be taken when the list being repeated contains only one element. Note that the expression 3 * 5 is a simple numeric computation, while ft. 3*[5]

[5, 5, 5]

produces a list containing the element 5 repeated 3 times. By surrounding a list to be repeated with an extra set of square brackets, lists consisting of other lists can be constructed:

ft. littlelist = [1,2,3]

ft. 3 * littlelist

[1, 2, 3, 1, 2, 3, 1, 2, 3]

>>> 3 * [littlelist]

[[1, 2, 3], [1, 2, 3], [1, 2, 3]]

4.3.3 The in operator

The in operator provides a very convenient way to determine if a particular value is contained in a list. As its name implies, you provide a value on the left hand side of the operator, and a list on the right hand side; an expression so constructed will return 1 if the value is in the list and 0 otherwise, making it ideal for conditional statements (Section 6.4). The left hand side can be a literal value, or an expression; the value on the right hand side can be a list, or an expression that evaluates to a list.

44 CHAPTER 4. LISTS, TUPLES AND DICTIONARIES

Since python's lists are so flexible, you need to be careful about how you construct expressions involving the in operator; only matches of the same type and value will return a value of 1. Consider the list squarepairs, each of whose elements are a list consisting of a small integer and its square:

>>> squarepairs = [[0,0],[1,1],[2,4],[3,9]]

To see if a list containing the elements 2 and 4 is contained in the squarepairs list, we could use an expression like the following:

ft. [2,4] in squarepairs

1

Python responds with a 1, indicating that such a list is an element of squarepairs. But notice that neither element of the list alone would be found in squarepairs:

ft. 2 in squarepairs

0

ft. 4 in squarepairs

0

The in operator works just as well with expressions that evaluate to elements in a list:

ft. nums = [0,1,2,3,4,5]

ft. [nums[2]] + [nums[4]] in squarepairs

1

The in operator is also used to iterate over the elements of a list in a for loop (Section 6.5).

4.4 Functions and Methods for Lists

As mentioned previously the len function will return the number of elements in a list. When called with a single list argument, the min function returns the smallest element of a list, and the max function returns the largest. When you provide more than one argument to these functions, the return the smallest (min) or largest (max) element among the arguments passed to the function.

The functions mentioned above accept a list as an argument, and return the desired result. However, many list operations are performed through methods instead of functions. Unlike strings (Section 2.4.4), lists are mutable objects, so many methods which operate on lists will change the list – the return value from the method should not be assigned to any object.

To add a single element to a list, use the append method. Its single argument is the element to be appended.

ft. furniture = ['couch','chair','table']

ft. furniture.append('footstool')

ft. furniture

['couch', 'chair', 'table', 'footstool']

If the argument to the append method is a list, then a single (list) element will be appended to the list to which the method is applied; if you need to add several elements to the end of a list, there are two choices. You can use the concatenation operator (Section 4.3.1) or the extend method. The extend method takes a single argument, which must be a list, and adds the elements contained in the argument to the end of a list. Notice the difference between invoking the extend and append methods in the following example:

ft. a = [1,5,7,9]

ft. b = [10,20,30,40]

ft. a.extend(b)

ft. a

[1, 5, 7, 9, 10, 20, 30, 40]

ft. a = [1,5,7,9]

ft. a.append(b)

ft. a

[1, 5, 7, 9, [10, 20, 30, 40]]

(Since the extend method changes the object on which it operates, it was necessary to reinitialize a before invoking the append method. An alternative would have been to use the copy function (Section 8.9) to make a copy of a for the second method.) Note that with extend, the elements of b were added to a as individual elements; thus the length of a is the total of its old length and the length of b, but when using append, b is added to a as a single element; the length of a list is always increased by exactly one when append operates on it.

46 CHAPTER 4. LISTS, TUPLES AND DICTIONARIES

In many cases we want to create a new list incrementally, by adding one element to the list at a time. As a simple example, suppose we have a list of numbers and we want to create a second list containing only those numbers which are less than 0. If we try to append an element to a non-existent list, it raises a NameError exception:

ft. oldlist = [7, 9, -3, 5, -8, 19]

ft. for i in oldlist:

... if i < 0 : newlist.append(i)

...

Traceback (innermost last):

File "<stdin>", line 2, in ?

NameError: newlist

(Don't worry if you don't understand the details of the for and if state-ments; they will be covered in Sections 6.5 and 6.4, respectively.) The solu-tion is to assign an empty list to newlist before we begin the loop. Such a list will have a length of zero, and no elements; the purpose of the assignment is simply to inform python that we will eventually refer to newlist as a list.

ft. oldlist = [7, 9, -3, 5, -8, 19]

ft. newlist = [ ]

ft. for i in oldlist:

... if i < 0 : newlist.append(i)

...

ft. newlist

[-3, -8]

To add an item to a list at a location other than the end, the insert method can be used. This method takes two arguments; the first is the index at which the item is to be inserted, and the second is the item itself. Note that only one element can be inserted into a list using this method; if you need to insert multiple items, slicing (Section 4.2) can be used.

To remove an item from a list, based on its value, not its subscript, python provides the remove method. It accepts a single argument, the value to be removed. Note that remove only removes the first occurence of a value from a list.

The reverse and sort methods perform their operations on a list in place; in other words, when these methods are invoked on a list, the ordering

4.4. FUNCTIONS AND METHODS FOR LISTS

47

of the elements in the list is changed, and the original ordering is lost. The methods do not return the reversed or sorted lists, so you should never set a list to the value returned by these methods! If you wish to retain the list with the elements in their original order, you should copy the list (using the copy module, not a regular assignment; see Section 6.1 and Section 8.9).

By default, the sort method sorts its numeric arguments in numerical order, and string arguments in alphabetical order Since a list can contain arbitrary objects, sort needs to be very flexible; it generally sorts scalar numeric values before scalar string values, and it sorts lists by first comparing their initial elements, and continuing through the available list elements until one list proves to be different than the other.

To sort in some other order than the method's default, a comparison function accepting exactly two arguments can be supplied as an argument to sort This function should be modeled on the built-in function cmp, which returns 1 if its first argument is greater than the second, 0 if the two argu-ments are equal, and -1 if the second argument is greater than the first. We'll look at function definitions in more detail later, but let's say we wish to sort strings, ignoring the case of the strings. The lower function in the string module can be used to return the lower case version of a string, and if we use that to compare pairs of values, the strings will be sorted without regard to case. We can write and use a function to do this comparison as follows:

```
>>> def nocase(a,b):
... return cmp(a.lower(),b.lower())
...
```

ft. names = ['fred','judy','Chris','Sam','alex','Heather']

ft. copynames = names[:]

ft. names.sort()

ft. names

['Chris', 'Heather', 'Sam', 'alex', 'fred', 'judy']

ft. names = copynames[:]

ft. names.sort(nocase)

ft. names

['alex', 'Chris', 'fred', 'Heather', 'judy', 'Sam']

The count method counts how many times a particular value appears in a list. It accepts a single argument which represents the value you're looking for, and returns the number of times that the value appears in the list.

48 CHAPTER 4. LISTS, TUPLES AND DICTIONARIES

The index method accepts a single argument, and, if that argument is found in the list, it returns the index (subscript) of its first occurence. If the value is not in the list, a ValueError exception is raised.

The following example demonstrates the use of count and index.

ft. food = ['spam','spam','spam','sausage','spam']

ft. food.count('spam')

4

ft. food.index('spam')

0

Even though "spam" appears four times in the food list, the index method always returns the index of the first occurence of the value only. If the index method fails to find the requested element, a ValueError exception is raised.

Related Modules : copy, array, struct

Related Exceptions : IndexError, ValueError

4.5 Tuple Objects

Tuples are very much like lists, except for one important difference. While lists are mutable, tuples, like strings, are not. This means that, once a tuple is created, its elements can't be modified in place. Knowing that a tuple is immutable, python can be more efficient in manipulating tuples than lists, whose contents can change at any time, so when you know you won't need to change the elements within a sequence, it may be more efficient to use a tuple instead of a list. In addition, there are a number of situations (argument passing and string formatting for example) where tuples are required.

Tuples are created in a similar fashion to lists, except that there is no need for square brackets surrounding the value. When the python inter-preter displays a tuple, it always surrounds it with parentheses; you can use parentheses when inputting a tuple, but it's not necessary unless the tuple is part of an expression. This creates a slight syntactic problem when creating a tuple with either zero or one element; python will not know you're creating a tuple. For an empty (zero-element) tuple, a pair of empty parentheseis (()) can be used. But surrounding the value with parentheses is not enough in the case of a tuple with exactly one element, since parentheses are used for grouping in arithmetic expression. To specify a tuple with only one element in an assignment statement, simply follow the element with a comma. In

arithmetic expressions, you need to surround it with parentheses, and follow the element with a comma before the closing parenthesis.

For example, suppose we wish to create a new tuple which concatenates the value 7 to the end of an existing tuple:

ft. values = 3,4,5

ft. values + (7)

Traceback (innermost last):
File "<stdin>", line 1, in ?
TypeError: illegal argument type for built-in operation

ft. values + (7,) (3, 4, 5, 7)

ft. newvalue = 7,

ft. values + newvalue (3, 4, 5, 7)

Without the closing comma, python regards the value (7) as just a single number, and raises a TypeError exception when we try to concatenate it to an existing tuple. The closing comma identifies the expression as a single-element tuple, and concatenation can be performed.

Like lists, the contents of tuples are arbitrary. The only difference is that lists are mutable and tuples are not.

4.6 Operators and Indexing for Tuples

The same operators mentioned in Section 4.3 for lists apply to tuples as well, keeping in mind that tuples are immutable. Thus, slicing operations for tuples are more similar to strings than lists; slicing can be used to extract parts of a tuple, but not to change them.

4.7 Functions and Methods for Tuples

Since tuples and lists are so similar, it's not surprising that there are times when you'll need to convert between the two types, without changing the values of any of the elements. There are two builtin functions to take care of this: list, which accepts a tuple as its single argument and returns a list with identical elements, and tuple which accepts a list and returns a tuple.

These functions are very useful for resolving TypeError exceptions involving lists and tuples.

There are no methods for tuples; however if a list method which doesn't change the tuple is needed, you can use the list function to temporarily change the tuple into a list to extract the desired information.

Suppose we wish to find how many times the number 10 appears in a tuple. The count method described in Section 4.4 can not be used on a tuple directly, since an AttributeError is raised:

ft. v = (7,10,12,19,8,10,4,13,10)

ft. v.count(10)

Traceback (innermost last):
File "<stdin>", line 1, in ?
AttributeError: 'tuple' object has no attribute 'count'

To solve the problem, call the list function with the tuple as its argument, and invoke the desired method directly on the object that is returned:

ft. list(v).count(10)

3

Note, however, that if you invoke a method which changes or reorders the values of a temporary list, python will not print an error message, but no change will be made to the original tuple.

ft. a = (12,15,9)

ft. list(a).sort()

ft. a

(12, 15, 9)

In case like this, you'd need to create a list, invoke the method on that list, and then convert the result back into a tuple.

ft. aa = list(a)

ft. aa.sort()

ft. a = tuple(aa)

ft. a

(9, 12, 15)

4.8 Dictionaries

Dictionaries (sometimes refered to as associative arrays or hashes) are very similar to lists in that they can contain arbitrary objects and can be nested to any desired depth, but, instead of being indexed by integers, they can be indexed by any immutable object, such as strings or tuples. Since humans can more easily associate information with strings than with arbitrary numbers, dictionaries are an especially convenient way to keep track of information within a program.

As a simple example of a dictionary, consider a phonebook. We could store phone numbers as tuples inside a list, with the first tuple element being the name of the person and the second tuple element being the phone number:

>>> phonelist = [('Fred','555-1231'),('Andy','555-1195'),('Sue','555-2193')]

However, to find, say, Sue's phone number, we'd have to search each element of the list to find the tuple with Sue as the first element in order to find the number we wanted. With a dictionary, we can use the person's name as the index to the array. In this case, the index is usually refered to as a key. This makes it very easy to find the information we're looking for:

ft. phonedict = {'Fred':'555-1231','Andy':'555-1195','Sue':'555-2193'}

ft. phonedict['Sue']

'555-2193'

As the above example illustrates, we can initialize a dictionary with a comma-separated list of key/value pairs, separated by colons, and surrounded by curly braces. An empty dictionary can be expressed by a set of empty curly braces ({}).

Dictionary keys are not limited to strings, nor do all the keys of a dic-tionary need be of the same type. However, mutable objects such as lists can not be used as dictionary keys and an attempt to do so will raise a TypeError. To index a dictionary with multiple values, a tuple can be used:

>>> tupledict = {(7,3):21,(13,4):52,(18,5):90}

Since the tuples used as keys in the dictionary consist of numbers, any tuple containing expressions resulting in the same numbers can be used to index the dictionary:

52 CHAPTER 4. LISTS, TUPLES AND DICTIONARIES

ft. tupledict[(4+3,2+1)]

21

In addition to initializing a dictionary as described above, you can add key/value pairs to a dictionary using assignment statements:

ft. tupledict[(19,5)] = 95

ft. tupledict[(14,2)] = 28

To eliminate a key/value pair from a dictionary use the del statement.

4.9 Functions and Methods for Dictionaries

As is the case for strings and lists, the len function returns the number of elements in a dictionary, that is, the number of key/value pairs. In addition, a number of methods for dictionaries are available.

Since refering to a non-existent key in a dictionary raises a KeyError exception, you should avoid indexing a dictionary unless you're sure of the existence of an entry with the key you are using. One alternative is to use a try/except clause (Section 1.4.5) to trap the KeyError. Two methods are also useful in this situation. The has_key method returns 1 (true) if the specified dictionary has the key which the method accepts as an argument, and 0 (false) otherwise. Thus, an if clause (Section 6.4) can be used to take action if a specified key does not exists. The get method also accepts a key as an argument, but it returns the value stored in the dictionary under that key if it exists, or an optional second argument if there is no value for the key provided. With only one argument, get returns the value

None when there is no value corresponding to the key provided.

As an illustration of these methods, suppose we are counting how many times a word appears in a file by using each word as a key to a dictionary called counts, and storing the number of times the word appears as the corresponding value. The logic behind the program would be to add one to the value if it already exists, or to set the value to one if it does not, since that will represent the first time the word is encountered. Here are three code fragments illustrating the different ways of handling a value stored in word which may or may not already be a key in the dictionary. (Remember that counts would have to be initialized to an empty dictionary before any elements could be added to it.)

4.9. FUNCTIONS AND METHODS FOR DICTIONARIES

53

- method 1: exceptions try:

  counts[word] = counts[word] + 1 except KeyError:
  counts[word] = 1

- method 2: check with has_key

  if counts.has_key(word):
  counts[word] = counts[word] + 1
  else:
  counts[word] = 1
  # method 3: use get
  counts[word] = counts.get(word,0) + 1

Although the third method is the shortest, it may not be obvious why it works. When an entry with the specified key already exists, the get method will return that entry and increment it by 1. If the key does not exist, the optional second argument to get forces it to return a value of 0, which, when incremented by 1 gives the correct initial value.

As of version 2.2, it is possible to iterate over a dictionary using a for loop; the operation will return the keys of the dictionary in an arbitrary order. In addition, the in operator can be used as an alternative to the has key method to determine if a particular key is present in a dictionary.

A few other methods provide alternative ways of accessing the keys, values or key/value pairs of a dictionary. The keys method returns a list of just the keys of a dictionary, and the values method returns a list of just the values. While the returned lists have their elements stored in an arbitrary order, corresponding elements in the two lists will be key/value pairs. The items method returns a list of tuples consisting of all the key/value pairs. Returning to the example using names as keys and phone numbers as values, here are the results of invoking these three methods on the phonedict dictionary:

ft. phonedict = {'Fred':'555-1231','Andy':'555-1195','Sue':'555-2193'}

ft. phonedict.keys()

['Fred', 'Sue', 'Andy']
>>> phonedict.values()
['555-1231', '555-2193', '555-1195']
54 CHAPTER 4. LISTS, TUPLES AND DICTIONARIES
>>> phonedict.items()
[('Fred', '555-1231'), ('Sue', '555-2193'), ('Andy', '555-1195')]

To remove all the elements of a dictionary, use the clear method. This differs from using the del operator on the dictionary in that the dictionary, although empty, still exists. To make a copy of a dictionary, use the copy method; remember that assignment of a dictionary to another variable may not do what you think (Section 6.1).

Python provides the update method to allow your to merge all the key/value pairs in one dictionary with those in another. If the original dictionary has an entry with the same key as one in the dictionary used for updating, the value from the dictionary used for updating will be placed in the original dictionary.

ft. master = {'orange':3,'banana':5,'grapefruit':2}

ft. slave = {'apple':7,'grapefruit':4,'nectarine':3}

ft. master.update(slave)

ft. master

{'banana': 5, 'orange': 3, 'nectarine': 3, 'apple': 7, 'grapefruit': 4}

Since both master and slave had entries for the key "grapefruit", the value found in master after the call to update is the one which was in slave.

Chapter 5Input and Output

5.1 The print command

The fastest way to print the value of an object in python is with the print command. You provide the command with a comma separated list of ob-jects, and it displays them with spaces between each object, and a newline added at the end. The newline can be supressed by terminating the print command with a comma. The print command is capable of producing a printed representation of any type of python object, but does not provide much control over the appearance of the output. Thus, it's ideal for quick interactive jobs or short programs where the appearance of the output is not critical.

For more control over the appearance of the output, you can first format the object you wish to print (Section 5.2); to direct output to a file, see Section 5.4

5.2 Formatting Strings

In python, string formatting is performed through overloading of the percent operator (%) for string values. On the left hand side of the operator, you provide a string which is a combination of literal text and formatting codes. Each appearance of a formatting code is matched with an object in a tuple, which appears on the right hand side of the percent sign. The resultant string (which is suitable for printing) replaces the formatting codes with formatted versions of the objects in the tuple. A brief description of the

55

56

CHAPTER 5. INPUT AND OUTPUT

Code

Meaning

d or i

Decimal Integer

u. Unsigned Integer o Octal Integer

h or H Hexadecimal Integer

f. Floating Point Number

e or E Floating Point Number: Exponential Notation
g or G Floating Point Number: "Optimal" Notation

s. String value - also provides string representation of any object c Single character

%Literal percent sign

Table 5.1: Formatting Codes

formatting codes is shown in Table 5.2. The formatting codes are preceded with a percent sign, and, optionally, a number which indicates the number of columns which should be used to format the value. For floating point numeric values, the percent sign can optionally be followed by two numbers separated by a period (.); in this case the first number is the field width, and the second number is the number of digits to display after the decimal point. For example, to produce a string called fstring which contains the number 7, formatted with three zeroes after the decimal point, we could use a statement like the following:

ft. fstring = 'The number is %5.3f' % (7)

ft. fstring

'The number is 7.000'

Notice that the field width was specified as 5, because it needs to be wide enough to display the number along with the decimal point.

The %g and %G formatting codes will use normal notation when the expo-nent of a number is greater than -4, and the specified width is sufficient to display the number. If either of these conditions is not true, then exponential notation will be used.

The right hand argument to the percent sign must contain a tuple, al-though parentheses are not strictly required when there is exactly one ar-gument to be formatted. With multiple items to be formatted, the format specifications and values are matched one-to-one.

5.3. USING NAMES IN FORMAT STRINGS

57

ft. print '%d items at %5.2f per item gives a total of $%4.2f' % \

... (7,.29,7 * .29)

7 items at 0.29 per item gives a total of $2.03

If you fail to provide the proper number of arguments to be converted, a TypeError is raised.

5.3 Using Names in Format Strings

As an alternative to the method described in the previous section, where the arguments to be formatted had to be in a tuple, python allows you to use a dictionary to contain the values to be formatted, and to use the dictionary's keys within the format string for added readability. To use this feature, put the appropriate key, surrounded in parentheses, between the percent sign and the format code of the appropriate element in the format string. For example, suppose the information to be formatted in the previous section was stored in a dictionary as follows:

>>> info = {'quantity':7,'itemprice':.29,'totalprice':7 * .29}

Then we could produce the same result as the previous example with the following print statement:

>>> print '%(quantity)d items at %(itemprice)5.2f ' \

... 'per item gives a total of $%(totalprice)4.2f' % info 7 items at 0.29 per item gives a total of $2.03

Notice that python concatenated the two pieces of the formatting string, due to the presence of the backslash at the end of the first line.

5.4 File Objects

In python, access to files is provided through a file object, which is created by calling the builtin open function. Once such an object is created, a large number of methods are available for accessing the file, both for reading and writing.

The open function takes between one and three arguments. The first, which is the only required argument, is the name of the file to open. The

58 CHAPTER 5. INPUT AND OUTPUT

String Meaning

r. Open file for reading; file must exist.

w. Open file for writing; will be created if it doesn't exist

a. Open file for appending; will be created if it doesn't exist r+ Open file for reading and writing; contents are not destroyed w+ Open file for reading and writing; contents are destroyed a+ Open file for reading and writing; contents are not destroyed

Table 5.2: File modes for the open function

second is a string which describes the action(s) that you plan to do to the file, as illustrated in Table 5.2. If you do not provide a second argument, the default is 'r', that is, the file is opened for reading. A 'b' can be appended to the second argument to indicate that the file to be opened is a binary file as opposed to a text file; this is only meaningful under operating systems like Windows which make a distinction between text files and binary files, and, when omitted, often causes problems when porting a program to such an operating system. Finally, the optional third argument specifies information about how the file should be buffered; a value of 0 means no buffering, a value of 1 means line buffering, and any other positive value indicates the size of the buffer to be used. (In this context, the buffer controls the amount of information that is manipulated in memory before any action is actually taken on the file.) In most cases, there should be no need to provide open with a third argument. Unfortunately, there is no way to unbuffer standard output inside an executing program; if you need standard output to be unbuffered, you must invoke python with the -u flag.

When specifying a filename under Windows, you can use a single back-slash (\), a double backslash (\\), or a single forward slash (/) as a file separator. A single backslash should be used with caution, because all of the backslashed sequences in Table 2.1 will still retain their usual meaning.

If python encounters a problem when opening a file, it will issue an IOError exception, along with a more detailed message describing the prob-lem. Thus, it is a wise practice to open files inside a try/except clause to prevent your program from terminating ungracefully when there's a problem opening a file.

Once you have successfully opened a file, there are a number of methods which can be invoked by the file object returned by open. The following

5.4. FILE OBJECTS

59

subsections describe some of these methods.

5.4.1 Methods for Reading

The readline method reads a single line from a file, including its terminating newline. (Under Windows, when Python reads text from a file, it discards the line feed which is on each line, leaving just a newline character.) To eliminate this newline, a common practice is to replace the read line with a string slice which eliminates the last character of the line:

ft. f = open('inputfile','r')

ft. line = f.readline()

ft. line

'Line one\012'

ft. line = line[:-1]

ft. line

'Line one'

Each call to the readline method will read the next line in the file until the contents of the file are exhausted; from that point on, python will return a completely empty string (i.e. no blanks or newlines), until the file is rewound (Section 5.4.4) or closed and reopened. If the goal is to process all of a file, however, you can iterate over each line of the file directly using a for loop (Section 6.5).

The readlines method reads an entire file in a single call and returns a list consisting of all of the lines in the file; each element of the list returned by readlines contains one line (including the terminating newline) from the file. Once the readlines method is invoked once, subsequent calls on the same file object will return an empty list, unless the file is rewound (Section 5.4.4) or closed and reopened.

The read method reads an entire file in a single call and returns the contents of the file in a scalar string variable, with newlines embedded within the string. An optional integer argument n limits the amount of data read to n bytes.

Note that the readlines and read methods both read the entire contents of a file into memory, and may cause problems when reading very large files.

60 CHAPTER 5. INPUT AND OUTPUT

5.4.2 Methods for Writing

Before discussing the available methods for writing to a file, remember that, in order to write to a file, the file must be opened with either the 'w' (write) or 'a' (append) modes. Furthermore, the objects to be written must be strings - no automatic conversion of of numbers to strings is carried out.

The write method takes a single scalar argument and writes it to the file represented by the file object on which it operates. Note that, unlike the print command, the write method does not automatically append a newline character to its argument. One consequence of this is that you can safely write binary files, or files with embedded null characters, using the write method. If you are writing a binary file, remember to append a 'b' to the second argument of the open function as described in Section 5.4.

The writelines method accepts a list argument, and writes each element of the list to the specified file as if a call to the write method had been made; no newlines are added to the output.

5.4.3 "Printing" to a File

Since the write method does not append a newline character to each line which it writes to a file, it is often inconvenient to convert a program which uses the print statement (which does append newlines) to one which will direct its output to a file. To make this easier, an extended form of the print statement was introduced in version 2 of python. To use this form, it is still necessary to create a file object which is opened for writing, but instead of invoking the write method, the file object can be specified on the print statement, preceded by two right brackets (>>), and followed by a comma. Thus, if we had a program which was designed to print to standard output with a statment like

print msg;

we could modify it to write to a file called "output.file" by first creating a file object suitable for writing:

try:

outfile = open('output.file','w')

except IOError:

print 'output.file could not be opened' sys.exit(1)

5.4. FILE OBJECTS

61

and then using the following print statement:

print >> outfile, msg;

5.4.4 Other Methods

The close method can be used to close a file after you are done reading or writing to it. While python will automatically close open files when you try to re-open them, and at the end of your program, it still is a good idea to explicitly close files when you are done using them.

When using buffered input or output, it may occasionally be useful to use the flush method to insure that the file's buffer is emptied.

The tell method returns the current offset of the file object in bytes. This is the location in the file where the next operation (read or write) will take place. To set the file pointer to a particular offset within the file, use the seek method. This method takes two arguments. The first is the desired offset (in bytes), and the second argument, which is optional, tells the system if the offset is from the beginning of the file (an argument of 0, the default), from the current position (an argument of 1) or from the end of the file (an argument of 2). A read or write operation following a call to seek will then be operating at the location specified. While there is no explicit "rewind" method provided, you can set the file offset to 0 for a file object f with the call

f.seek(0)

effectively setting the file back to the beginning.

The truncate method accepts a number of bytes as its argument and changes the length of the file being operated on to that many bytes. If the file is shorter than the number of bytes specified, it will be padded with null characters (binary zeroes, not blanks).

5.4.5 File Object Variables

Along with the methods described above, file objects also contain several variables, often refered to as attributes, containing information about the file which the file object represents. These attributes are accessed just like methods, except that, since they are variables, they accept no arguments, and need no parentheses when accessed. The name attribute is a character

62 CHAPTER 5. INPUT AND OUTPUT

string containing either the name of the file or a description of its source. The closed attribute is an integer variable which is 1 if the file is closed, and 0 if the file is open. The mode attribute is a variable containing a character string, similar to the one passed to open indicating the mode through which the file was opened. Each of these attributes is read-only, and attempts to change them will result in a TypeError.

5.5 Standard Input and Output Streams

In a UNIX-style operating system, there are three so-called "streams", which represent file-like objects through which input to and output from programs is directed. The stream known as standard input generally represents the keyboard and is the basic source of user input to text-based programs. The streams known as standard output and standard error are the default desti-nations for output from programs, and generally represent the screen of the user's computer. For many simple tasks, Python provides functions so that you don't have to deal with these streams directly. For example, the print statement directs its output to the standard output stream; the raw input function reads its input from the standard input stream. Using these func-tions, you can establish a simple dialog with a user:

```
name = raw_input('What is your name? ')
flavor = raw_input('What is your favorite ice cream flavor? ')
print 'Hi, %s, I like %s too' % (name,flavor)
```

The raw input function writes its argument to standard output (usually the computer screen), reads a line from standard input (usually the keyboard), strips the trailing newline from the response, and returns it.

Even for more complex use of the standard streams, there is no need to explicitly open or close them; they are defined as file object attributes of the sys module with the names stdin for standard input, stderr for standard error, and stdout for standard output. Since they are defined as file objects, they can be manipulated like any other file. For example, it is often useful to read the input for a program from a file name if one is provided on a command line, or from the keyboard (standard input) if no file name is provided. The following program checks to see if a filename is given on the command line by examining the length of the argv variable of the system]module, and

5.6. PIPES

63

then decides whether to take its input from a file or from the standard input. (See Section 8.8 for more information about argv.)

```
import sys
if len(sys.argv) > 1:
try:
f = open(sys.argv[1],'r')
except IOError:
print >>sys.stderr, 'Error opening %s\n' % sys.argv[1] sys.exit(1)
else:
f = sys.stdin
while 1:
line = f.readline()
...
```

Since sys.stdin is just a file object, reading from standard input is no different than reading from any other file. Notice that the error message from the program was directed to standard error, and not standard output. When you're writing a program and you wish to produce an error message, it's a good idea to write the error message to the stderr stream rather than relying on the default behaviour of the print command (which is to write to stdout). When you use stderr, error messages will still appear on the user's screen, even if they have redirected the standard output stream to a file.

Since the sys.stdout stream is already open when you invoke python, it is not possible to pass a third argument to open (See Section 5.4) in order to make output to this stream unbuffered. If you need sys.stdout to be unbuffered (so that, for example, redirected output is written immediately instead of waiting until a buffer is filled), you can invoke python with the -u option (/u under Windows).

5.6 Pipes

Sometimes, instead of reading input from a file, it's necessary to read input which comes from an program. For example, many operating system com-

64 CHAPTER 5. INPUT AND OUTPUT

mands produce output which is not in a very convenient format; one of the important uses of languages like python is to be able to extract useful infor-mation from such commands, and present it in an appropriately formatted way. Similarly, it is very useful to be able to have python send its output to a command. For example, you may need to perform a statistical analysis by having python gather data and then send it to a program to perform the analysis. When you read output from a command or send output to a com-mand the input stream to your program is known as a pipe. In python, you can open a pipe using the popen function of the os module So somewhere near the beginning of your program you need a line like

import os

to import the entire os module or

from os import popen

to bring just popen into the local namespace. In the examples that follow, I'll assume that the entire module has been imported. While this may not be the most efficient route, one benefit is that it's always very clear where a function like popen is coming from, since it needs to be refered to as os.popen.

One benefit of object-oriented programming is that, if the object returned by os.popen is designed to support the same methods as a file object, then the only difference between working with files and working with pipes is that different functions are used to initially create the objects on which these methods are invoked. This is exactly the way a pipe object is designed. Furthermore, the arguments to os.popen are exactly the same as those to the built-in open command, except that the first argument to os.popen is interpreted as an operating system command instead of a file name.

For example, suppose we want to read the output of the UNIX df com-mand, which provides information about the space being used on a com-puter's hard drives. The output of the command might look something like this:

Filesystem

1024-blocks Used Available Capacity

Mounted on

/dev/hda1

1398534 1102892

223370

83%

/

/dev/hdb1

2970455 2060577

756261

73%

/new

/dev/hdb2

2970487 2540561
276307
90%

/new1
5.6. PIPES

65

The goal of the program would be to add together the three columns which provide the amount of information about the drives and print a total for each column, along with an overall percentage of the capacity of the drives.

After opening a pipe to the command with os.popen, we can break apart each line and extract the numbers, add them together, and report the desired information:

```
import os,sys
try:
df = os.popen('df -k','r')
except IOError:
stderr.write('Couldn\'t run df command\n')
sys.exit(1)
tot = used = avail = 0
while 1:
line = df.readline()
if not line : break
line = line[:-1]
if line[:10] == 'Filesystem' : continue parts = line.split()[1:] tot = tot + int(parts[0])
used = used + int(parts[1])
avail = avail + int(parts[2])
    print 'Total: %d Used: %d Avail: %d Capacity %2.0f%%' % \ (tot,used,avail,float(used)/float(tot) * 100.)
```

If the program was stored in a file called df.py, and was made executable, it would produce the following output:

```
% df.py
Total: 7339476 Used: 5704030 Avail: 1255938 Capacity 78%
```

66 CHAPTER 5. INPUT AND OUTPUT

Chapter 6 Programming

6.1 Assignments

One of the basic operations in any computer language is the assignment statement. The assignment statement allows us to associate a variable name with a value, so we can more easily manipulate our data. In python, like many other languages, the equal sign (=) is used to assign a value to a variable; the variable name is put on the left hand side of the equal sign, and the value (any valid python expression) is put on the right hand side of the equal sign. Some simple examples of assignment statements follow:

ft. x = 3

ft. y = 'This is a string'

ft. z = x + 3

ft. y = abs(-7)

ft. vegies = ['broccoli','peas','carrots']

ft. meal = vegies

Assignment statements can be chained; if you need to set several variables to the same value, you can simply extend the assignment to each of the variables in a single statement:

>>> count = number = check = 0

All three variables (count, number, and check) will have the value 0 after this assignment. Note that, when using the python interpreter interactively, these assignment statements don't produce any output. (Of course, you can simply

67

68 CHAPTER 6. PROGRAMMING

type the name of any variable of interest, and its value will be displayed in interactive mode.)

Another handy feature of the assignment operator in python is that it supports multiple assignments. If you have a comma separated list of vari-ables on the left hand side of the equal sign, and an equal number of comma separated expressions on the right hand side, python assigns each variable to its corresponding expression:

ft. zero,one,ten = 0,1,10

ft. all = first,last = ['john','smith']

The second example shows how the ideas of chaining and multiple assign-ment can be combined; the variable first has the value "john", second has the value "smith", and all is a list containing the two values. This sort of technique can be used with any expression that evaluates to a sequence (string, list or tuple).

While the internal details of python should usually not concern you, there is one aspect of the assignment statement which needs to be understood to program effectively in python. Consider the following assignment statements:

- assignment of values

>>> x = 3
>>> z = x + 4
>>> breakfast = 'spam'
>>> names = ['Fred','Sam','Harry']

- assignments using variables

ft. friends = names

ft. y = x

ft. meal = breakfast

In the first set of assignments, the values for the assignment consisted of literal strings, numbers or lists, or expressions involving such quantities. In these cases, those values are stored in memory, and will be associated with their assigned names until you actively change them, or python is finished with your program.

But when you make assignments of one variable name to another, python actually stores a reference to the variable, that is, instead of creating a new copy of the contents of the original variable, it stores information about where the original variable is stored, and, when the new variable is later referenced,

6.1. ASSIGNMENTS

it goes back to this location to find the value of the variable. Thus, the statement

>>> x = 3

tells python to store the integer value 3 in a location associated with the variable name x, but the statement

>>> y = x

tells python to store the location of the variable x in the variable y, and to use the value stored at that location as the value of y. This is one of several design features of python that help to keep the language efficient. To prevent you from losing your data, python keeps track of how many times a variable is referenced, and, if you change the value of a variable to which another variable has a reference, it copies the variable's value before it destroys it, so that the variable referencing it will continue to have the value you would expect it to have.

With scalar variables, it would be difficult to construct a situation where this scheme would produce surprising results, since once a reference's value is changed, python automatically updates the values of any variables which were referring to that value. With mutable objects such as lists, however, changes within the list do not initiate this updating mechanism, and sur-prising results can occur.

To illustrate, suppose we create a scalar variable, and assign it to a second variable:

ft. sound = 'Ni'

ft. knight = sound

If we change the value of the variable sound, python will update the value of knight so that the value is not lost:

ft. sound = 'Arf'

ft. sound

'Arf'

ft. knight 'Ni'

Now consider the case of a list. We'll create a list, then assign it to another variable:

70 CHAPTER 6. PROGRAMMING

ft. foods = ['spam','spam','spam','sausage','spam']

ft. meal = foods

If we assign an entirely new value to foods, python will update the value of meal so that it contains the original list, since it is now the only variable refering to that original list:

ft. foods = ['beans','spam','eggs']

ft. meal

['spam', 'spam', 'spam', 'sausage', 'spam']

But if we modify only part of the list, python will retain the reference so that meal will have the value of the modified list:

ft. foods = ['spam','spam','spam','sausage','spam']

ft. meal = foods

ft. foods[1] = 'beans'

ft. foods

```
['spam', 'beans', 'spam', 'sausage', 'spam']
>>> meal
['spam', 'beans', 'spam', 'sausage', 'spam']
```

Even though we didn't explicitly change any of the values stored through the name meal, you can see that meal is still refering to the (now modified) list stored under the name foods.

Python provides some tools to help you deal with this situation. The copy module (Section 8.9) provides a function called copy which will actually make a copy of a list, instead of simply storing a reference. Thus, if we wanted to insure that meal contained the original elements of foods even if foods got modified, we could invoke this function instead of using an assignment:

ft. import copy

ft. foods = ['spam','spam','spam','sausage','spam']

ft. meal = copy.copy(foods)

ft. foods[1] = 'beans'

ft. foods

```
['spam', 'beans', 'spam', 'sausage', 'spam']
>>> meal
['spam', 'spam', 'spam', 'sausage', 'spam']
```

6.1. ASSIGNMENTS

71

A similar result can be obtained by assigning a slice of an array where no starting or ending index is provided. Instead of calling the copy function, we could have made a true copy of foods in meal with a statement like

```
>>> meal = foods[:]
```

The is operator can be used to find out if one variable is a reference to another. Like the logical equals operator (==, Section 6.3), the is operator returns 1 or 0 depending on whether or not the two objects being compared are actually references to the same thing. (The equals operator simply checks to see if they are of the same type, and contain the same values.) We can study the behavior of the is operator by inserting a few additional statements in the above example:

ft. foods = ['spam','spam','spam','sausage','spam']

ft. meal1 = foods

ft. meal2 = copy.copy(foods)

ft. foods == meal1

1

ft. foods is meal1

1

ft. foods == meal2

1

ft. foods is meal2

0

ft. foods[1] = 'beans'

ft. foods == meal1

1

ft. foods is meal1

1

ft. foods == meal2

0

ft. foods is meal2

0

When a list is copied to another variable, its contents are identical to the original variable; thus the test for equality is true (i.e. 1). But since the contents of foods were actually copied to meal2, meal2 is not a reference to foods, and the is operator returns a false value (i.e. 0).

72 CHAPTER 6. PROGRAMMING

6.2 Indentation

Unlike most programming languages, where indentation is used simply to improve readability of programs, python uses indentation to signal the be-ginning and end of blocks of statements, that is, groups of statements which will be executed together based on the value of some condition, or the occur-rence of an exception. The first statement of your programs must start in the very first column, and within each indented block, you must be consistent in the amount of indentation you use. Although not strictly required, most python programmers try to be consistent in their indentation from block to block as well. The task of writing properly indented programs is made much easier if you use an editor which is python-aware; emacs and vim are examples of such editors, as well as the IDLE or pythonwin programming environments supplied as part of python distributions.

Although it takes some getting used to, using identation to group state-ments together has some definite benefits. Since there are no brackets or keywords involved in delineating blocks of statements, no decisions need to be made as to whether the delineators should appear on the same line as program statements, or if they should line up with the beginnings or ends of blocks. The result of this is that most python programs look very simi-lar, even if they were written by different people, making "foreign" python programs much easier to read and understand. In addition, since the in-dentation of a program actually determines its structure, python programs provide easy-to-see visual clues to help you understand what a program is doing.

6.3 Truth, Falsehood and Logical Operators

When you write a program and need to execute statements only under certain conditions, the if statement (Section 6.4) can be used; similarly, when you want to repeatedly execute commands until some condition becomes true or false, the while statement (Section 6.7) can be used. But before looking at the mechanics of these statements, it's important to understand python's ideas of what is true and false.

In python, numeric values are false if they are equal to zero, and true otherwise; sequence objects (like strings and lists) are false if they contain no elements, and are true otherwise. Similarly, a dictionary is false if it has no

Operator	Tests for
Operator	Tests for
==	Equality
!=	Non-equality
>	Greater than
<	Less than
>=	Greater than or equal
<=	Less than or equal
in	Membership in sequence
is	Equivalence
not in	Lack of membership
not is	Non-equivalence

Table 6.1: Comparison Operators

keys or values and is true otherwise. Finally, the special python value None also evaluates to false. It should be noted that, while assignment statements do evaluate to a value, they can not be used as tests in if or while loops. Because of this, it is very common in python to use a so-called "infinite" loop, where the argument of a while clause is set to 1, and break statements are used to insure that the loop will be properly terminated. (See Section 6.7 for details)

More commonly, however, logical expressions are created using binary comparison operators. These operators return 0 if the test they represent is false, and 1 if the test is true. They are summarized in Table 6.1.

You can combine logical expressions with the keywords and or or. When you combine two logical expressions with an and, both of the statements being combined must be true for the overall expression to be considered true. When you use an or to combine two statements, the overall statement is true if either of the statements being combined are true. You can use as many ands and ors as you need to create expressions to test for complex conditions, and you can freely use parentheses to make sure that python understands exactly what you mean.

One subtlety of the logical expressions has to do with what are often called side effects. For reasons of efficiency, python will only evaluate a logi-cal expression (from left to right) until it can determine whether or not the expression is true. What this means is that if you combine two logical ex-pressions with an and, python will never even evaluate the second expression if the first expression is false, because, once the first expression is false, the value of the second expression doesn't matter — overall, the combined ex-pression must be false. Similarly, if you combine two logical expressions with an or, then if the first expression is true, the second expression isn't eval-uated, since the combined expression must be true regardless of the second

74 CHAPTER 6. PROGRAMMING

expression's value. This can lead to strange behavior of your programs if you're not prepared for it.

Suppose we have a character string and we want to count the number of words in the string, but only if the length of the string is greater than

5. In the code that follows, I'm purposely making an error. I'm refering to the split function of the string module without properly importing the module:

ft. str = 'one'

ft. if len(str) > 5 and len(split(str,' ')) > 3:

...print 'too many words'

...

When I run this program, I don't see any error, even though I purposely refered to the split function which had not been properly imported. If the length of the string is greater than 5 however, the second part of the logical expression must be evaluated, and python informs us of the error:

ft. str = 'one two three four'

ft. if len(str) > 5 and len(split(str,' ')) > 3:

...print 'too many words'

...

Traceback (innermost last): File "<stdin>", line 1, in ?

NameError: split

The moral of this example is that it's important to understand python's logic when it evaluates logical expressions, and to realize that not all of the code in your logical expressions will actually be executed every time that it's encountered.

6.4 if statement

The if statement, along with optional elif and/or else statements is the basic tool in python for performing conditional execution. The basic form of the statement can be summarized as:

if expression :
statement(s)

6.4. IF STATEMENT

75

elif expression:
statement(s)
elif expression:

statement(s)

...

else:

statements

Python evaluates the expression after the if, and, if it is true, carries out the statement(s) which follow; if it is not true, it proceeds to the elif statement (if there is one), and tests that expression. It continues testing the expressions associated with any elif statements, and, once it finds an expression that is true, it carries out the corresponding statement(s) and jumps to the statement following the end of the if block. If it doesn't encounter any true expressions after trying all the elif clauses, and there is an else statement present, it will execute the statements associated with the else; otherwise, it just continues with the statement following the if block. Notice that once python encounters a true expression associated with an if or elif statement, it carries out the statements associated with that if or elif, and doesn't bother to check any other expressions. One implication of this is that if you need to test a number of possibilities where only one can be true, you should always use a set of if/elif clauses so that no extra work is done once the true expression has been found. For example, suppose we wish to do one of three different tasks depending on whether a variable x has the value 1, 2, or 3. Notice the subtle difference between these two pieces of code:

- first method - execution stops once the correct choice is found if x == 1:

```
z = 1
print 'Setting z to 1' elif x == 2:
y = 2
print 'Setting y to 2' elif x == 3:
w = 3
print 'Setting w to 3'
```

- second method - all three tests are done regardless of x's value if x == 1:

76 CHAPTER 6. PROGRAMMING

```
z = 1
print 'Setting z to 1'
if x == 2:
y = 2
print 'Setting y to 2'
if x == 3:
w = 3
print 'Setting w to 3'
```

Since x can only have one value, there's no need to test its value once the appropriate task is performed.

6.5 for loops

The for loop allows you to iterate over all the values in a sequence (string, list or tuple), performing the same task on each of the elements. In addition, starting with version 2.0, it's possible to iterate over other objects, such as file objects or dictionaries. The basic form of the for loop is:

```
for var in sequence:
statements
else:
statements
```

As with the if statement, there must be a colon at the very end of the for statement. The variable var is a "dummy" variable; its value is defined locally with the for loop, but when the for loop is completed, it will be equal to the last element in the sequence being processed.

Unlike the for statement, where the else (or elif) clause is often used, the optional else clause of the for loop is rarely used. The statements following the else statement are executed when the complete sequence of iterations defined by the for loop is completed. If a break statement (Sec-tion 6.8) is encountered inside the for loop, however, these statements are not carried out, and control goes to the next executable statement after the body of the for/else loop.

If the elements of the sequence being iterated over contain tuples or lists of a common size, you can replace var with a comma separated list representing the unpacking of each individual element of sequence. While this doesn't

really provide any new capabilities to the for loop, it does add a certain amount of convenience when processing sequences of this sort.

Suppose we have a sequence of tuples containing the last name and first names of people, and we wish to print the first names followed by the last names. Since the for loop lets us iterate over the elements of a sequence, and, in this case, the sequence consists of tuples of length two, we could access the names as follows:

```
ft. names = [('Smith','John'),('Jones','Fred'),('Williams','Sue')]

ft. for i in names:

... print '%s %s' % (i[1],i[0])
...
John Smith
Fred Jones
Sue Williams
```

By using the tuple unpacking feature of the for loop, we can express the same idea in an easier to understand form:

```
>>> for last,first in names:
... print '%s %s' % (first,last)
...
John Smith
Fred Jones
Sue Williams
```

As an example of iterating over a non-sequence, consider the file object introduced in Section 5.4. Once you've created a file object suitable for reading, iterating over the object will advance to the next line in the file. So to find the longest line in a file, you could use a for loop like the following:

```
try:
f = open('some.file','r')
except IOError:
print >>sys.stderr, "Couldn't open %s" % 'some.file' sys.exit(1)
maxlen = 0
for line in f:
l = len(line)
```



```
if l > maxlen:
maxlen = l
print 'Maximum length = %d' % maxlen
```

6.6 for loops and the range function

The for loop is very handy for processing a sequence of values, but there are several very common problems which the for loop can't handle by itself. First, changing the value of the for loop variable (var) does not change the value of the corresponding element in sequence. For example, suppose we tried to change the value of each element in an array to zero by using the for loop variable on the left-hand side of an assignment statement:

ft. x = [1,2,3,4,5]

ft. for i in x:

...i = 0

...

ft. x

[1, 2, 3, 4, 5]

The value of the elements in x was not changed, because the for loop vari-able represents only a copy of the value of the corresponding element in the sequence, not the actual element itself. Notice that if the elements of the sequence being iterated over are mutable objects, then elements stored within those objects can be changed by refering to the appropriate element of the loop variable. Consider the following array, whose elements are each another array. We could replace the first element of each of the array elements with zero using a for loop:

ft. dblarray = [[7,12,9],[13,8,3],[19,2,14]]

ft. for d in dblarray:

... d[0] = 0

...

>>> dblarray

[[0, 12, 9], [0, 8, 3], [0, 2, 14]]

Another example is the case of creating a new sequence by processing one or more other sequences. Suppose we have an array of prices and an

6.6. FOR LOOPS AND THE RANGE FUNCTION

79

array of the same length containing taxes, and we wish to create a third array which has the total of the prices and the taxes for each of the items represented in the two arrays. Clearly, the for loop as presented so far has no means of dealing with this problem. If you're familiar with other programming languages, you'll notice that these two tasks are quite simple in most other languages, at the cost of either a complex syntax or additional looping constructs.

In python, problems like this are solved by iterating over a sequence of integers created by the range function, and then refering to the individual elements of the sequence inside the body of the for loop to perform the desired tasks. The range function accepts one, two or three arguments. With a single integer argument, range returns a sequence of integers from 0 to one less than the argument provided. With two arguments, the first argument is used as a starting value instead of 0, and with three arguments, the third argument is used as an increment instead of the implicit default of 1. Notice that range never includes its upper limit in the returned sequence; like slices (Section 2.4.3), it is designed to work in conjunction with the subscripting of elements in a sequence, which start at 0 and continue to one less than the length of the sequence.

So to zero out all the elements in an array, we could use the range as follows:

ft. x = [1,2,3,4,5]

ft. for i in range(len(x)):

...x[i] = 0

...

ft. x

[0, 0, 0, 0, 0]

Since the len function returns the number of elements in a sequence, and since subscripts start with 0, range and len work very well together. Here's one solution to the problem of adding together an array of prices and taxes to create a total array:

ft. prices = [12.00,14.00,17.00]

ft. taxes = [0.48,0.56,0.68]

ft. total = []

ft. for i in range(len(prices)):

... total.append(prices[i] + taxes[i])

80 CHAPTER 6. PROGRAMMING

...

>>> total

[12.48, 14.56, 17.68]

Alternatively, we could refer to the elements of total with the same sub-scripts as the corresponding elements of prices and taxes, but we would first have to initialize total to have the correct number of elements:

ft. total = len(prices) * [0]

ft. for i in range(len(prices)):

... total[i] = prices[i] + taxes[i]

...

>>> total

[12.48, 14.56, 17.68]

The brackets around the 0 are required so that python will create a list with the appropriate number of elements, rather than a scalar (Section 4.3.2).

The range function actually produces a list in memory containing all the elements specified through its arguments. For sequences involving very large numbers, this may consume large amounts of memory. In cases like this, python provides the xrange function. While this function returns an object that behaves just like the list returned by range, the appropriate elements are calculated as needed, rather than actually stored in memory. Since this makes xrange considerably slower than range, you should only resort to xrange when working with a large range of values.

6.7 while loops

While the for loop provides an excellent way to process the elements of a sequence, there are times when it's necessary to do some repetitive compu-tation which is not based on an array. In those cases, the while loop can be used. The basic syntax of the while loop is as follows:

while expression:

statements
else:
statements
6.7. WHILE LOOPS

81

When python encounters a while loop, it firsts tests the expression provided; if it is not true, and an else clause is present, the statements following the else are executed. With no else clause, if the expression is not true, then control transfers to the first statement after the while loop.

If the expression is true, then the statements following the while state-ment are executed; when they are completed, the expression is tested once again, and the process is repeated. As long as the expression is true, execution of the statements after the while while be repeated; if the expression is not true, the statements after the else, if present, are executed. It should be noted that, as with the for loop, the else clause is not used very often with while loops, although there are situations where it can be used effectively.

To illustrate the while loop, consider an iterative process to calculate the cube root of a number. It's not necessary to understand the underlying math (based on Newton's method); it suffices to understand that, starting from an initial guess, we can calculate a new, better guess through a simple computation. But instead of repeating the process a fixed number of times (which could easily be accommodated by a for loop), we want to continue refining our guess until our answer is reasonably close to the correct one. In the case of calculating the cube root, a convenient criteria is that the absolute difference between the number we're working with and our guess cubed is small, say 1.e-8. The following python program uses a while loop to iteratively perform the calculation:

ft. num = 7.

ft. oldguess = 0.

ft. guess = 3.

ft. while abs(num - guess**3) > 1.e-8:

```
...oldguess = guess
... guess = oldguess - (oldguess**3 - num) / (3 * oldguess**2)
...
>>> guess
1.91293118277
```

ft. guess**3

7.0

Notice that the variables num, guess, and oldguess were all assigned values with decimal points included, to insure that calculations done with them would use floating point arithmetic as opposed to integer arithmetic (Section 3.1).

82 CHAPTER 6. PROGRAMMING

A common practice in many languages is to assign a value to a variable by calling a function which returns a non-zero value when it is successful, and a value of zero when it fails. This assignment is then used as the expression of a while loop. In python, this practice is not permitted, for a number of reasons. First, most python functions communicate failure by throwing an exception, not by returning a zero or None value. Furthermore, since an assignment (=) can so easily be mistaken for a test for equality (==) or vice versa, this practice often leads to very difficult-to-track bugs in your programs. For this reason, programming of while loops is often different in python than in other languages. In particular, since assignments can't be used as expressions in while loops, many python programmers write while loops as so-called "infinite" loops, and determine when to stop executing the loop through programming statements inside the loop using the techniques described in the next section.

6.8 Control in Loops: break and continue

In order to decide when to stop executing a while loop from within the body of the loop, instead of the expression provided with the while statement, python provides the break statement. When you issue a break statement inside a loop (for or while), control is immediately transfered to the first statement after the body of the loop, including any elif or else clauses which are attached. Thus, the else clause of a while statement is executed only after the expression of the while loop is tested and found to be false. The statements following the else are not executed if control is transfered from the while clause through a break statement.

Before the introduction of iterators in version 2.0, a common use of the break statement was to reading data from a file line by line. This technique is still useful if a file-like object does not support iteration.

```
try:
f = open('filename','r')
except IOError,msg:
print 'Error opening filename: %s' % (msg[1])
sys.exit(1)
while 1:
```



```
line = f.readline()
if not line : break
```

- continue processing input line

Since assignments aren't allowed as while loop expressions, the value of 1, which is always guaranteed to be true, is used as the expression of the while loop; thus it is essential that a break statement is used somewhere in the body of the loop to insure that execution will eventually terminate. Here, we terminate execution of the loop when the readline method returns a value of None, signaling that it has reached the end of the file. Obviously, in loops of this sort, an else clause would never make sense, since the loop will never exit due to the while loop's expression taking on a false value.

The continue statement can be used in either for or while loops to instruct python to continue on to the next iteration of the loop without executing the statements in the loop which follow the continue statement. In a for loop, the value of the loop variable is incremented after a continue statement, so that after skipping the remaining part of the loop for the current iteration, the next iteration will be performed in the normal fashion.

Often a continue statement can be used as an alternative to an if state-ment inside a loop, and it's just a matter of personal preference as to which one is used. For example, suppose we wish to find the largest number in an array, as well as the index within the array at which the largest value occured. Using a continue statement, we could use the following:

ft. x = [7, 12, 92, 19, 18 ,44, 31]

ft. xmax = x[0]

ft. imax = 0

ft. for i in range(1,len(x)):

... if x[i] <= xmax : continue
... xmax = x[i]
... imax = i
...

ft. print 'Maximum value was %d at position %d.' % (xmax,imax) Maximum value was 92 at position 2.

Similar results could be obtained by putting the last two statements of the for loop as the clause of an if statement to be carried out when a new maximum value is found:

84 CHAPTER 6. PROGRAMMING

ft. for i in range(1,len(x)):

...if x[i] > xmax:
... xmax = x[i]
... imax = i
...

ft. print 'Maximum value was %d at position %d.' % (xmax,imax) Maximum value was 92 at position 2.

6.9 List Comprehensions

When you're using a for loop to process each element of a list, you can sometimes use a construction known as a list comprehension, which was introduced into version 2.0 of python, to simplify the task. The basic format of a list comprehension is

[expression for var-1 in seq-1 if condition-1 for var-2 in seq-2 if condition-2 ...]

and the returned value is a list containing expression evaluated at each combination of var-1, var-2,. . . which meets the if conditions, if any are present. The second and subsequent for's, and all of the if's are optional. For example, suppose we wanted to create a list containing the squared values of the elements in some other list. We could use a for loop in the following way:

ft. oldlist = [7,9,3,4,1,12]

ft. newlist = []

ft. for i in oldlist:

... newlist.append(i*i)
...
>>> newlist
[49, 81, 9, 16, 1, 144]

Using a list comprehension, we can express this more succinctly:

>>> newlist = [i * i for i in oldlist]

By using if clauses within the list comprehension, we can be more selective about the elements we return:

6.9. LIST COMPREHENSIONS

85

ft. [i * i for i in oldlist if i % 2 == 1] [49, 81, 9, 1]

When you have more than one for clause, all possible combinations of the variables in the for clauses will be evaluated:

>>> [(x,y) for x in range(3) for

y in range(4)]

[(0, 0), (0, 1), (0, 2), (0, 3),

(1, 0), (1,

1), (1, 2), (1, 3), (2, 0), (2, 1), (2, 2),

(2, 3)]

if clauses can be added after either of the for clauses; to refer to combina-tions involving all the variables, use an if clause at the very end:

ft. [(x,y) for x in range(3) if x in (1,2) for y in range(4) if y == 0] [(1, 0), (2, 0)]

ft. [(x,y) for x in range(3) for y in range(4) if x + y < 3]

[(0, 0), (0, 1), (0, 2), (1, 0), (1, 1), (2, 0)]

86 CHAPTER 6. PROGRAMMING

Chapter 7 Functions

7.1 Introduction

Functions are an important part of any programming language for two rea-sons. First, they allow you to reuse code you've written, without the need to copy and modify the code each time you use it. For example, if you are working with a data base, you'll always need to make a connection to the data base, and inform it of the table you want to access. By writing a func-tion to do this, you can dispose of the task with a single line of code in every program that needs to access the data base. An added advantage to using a function for a task like this is that if you ever need to change the type of data base you're using, or if you detect a flaw in the logic you used when you first wrote the function, you can simply edit a single version of the function, and other programs can simply import the corrected version to be instantly updated.

The second reason to use functions is that it allows you to logically isolate the different sub-tasks which invariably emerge when you're working on a program. In the database example, you'd generally need to connect to the database, and then either query the database or make some changes. By writing one function to connect, a second to query and a third to update, you can write the main part of your program very concisely, and study its logic without having to get into the details of the database itself. Debugging such a program becomes much simpler because, once a set of functions has been developed and tested, it's not hard to figure out whether a problem is arising from one of the functions, or from the code that's calling it.

88 **CHAPTER 7. FUNCTIONS**

This style of programming is known as modular programming, and is generally recognized as a useful way to make writing easy-to-read and maintainable programs.

In Python, functions are just one more type of object. Thus you can assign a function to another name, store them in lists or tuples, pass them to other functions, and so on. But they have one special property which sets them apart from most other Python objects: when you provide them with a list of arguments surrounded by parentheses, they can perform some task, using the arguments as a guide as to what they should do, and, optionally they can return a value, which can be used like any other value of the same type.

We've already seen a number of functions in previous chapters, such as len (Section 2.4.4), which returns the length of a sequence such as a string or a list, and min and max (Section 4.4), which return the minimum or maximum value contained in a sequence. We've also encountered many methods, which are very similar to functions, and defined in basically the same way.

In this chapter we'll examine some of the issues surrounding functions and how to create functions and import them into your programs.

7.2 Scoping: How Python finds your vari-ables

When you write a program in Python, you can generally refer to variables anywhere in the program and Python will find the appropriate values. But when you create a function, it could potentially be dangerous for Python to treat the variables within a function as equivalent to the ones which were used outside the function. Consider this simple example of a function, which adds all the values in a list:

```
def addem(list):
sum = 0.
for i in list:
sum = sum + i
return sum
```

If Python didn't provide some mechanism for "private" variables within func-tions, every time you called the addem function, the variable i would get over-written by the last value in the list being processed by the function. When

7.2. SCOPING: HOW PYTHON FINDS YOUR VARIABLES

89

you define a function, Python creates a separate namespace within that func-tion A namespace is a mapping between object names in your program and the location in memory where Python actually stores their values. So when you create a variable inside a function, Python understands that you mean the local variable in the function's name space, and not a variable of the same name defined somewhere else. Thus, in the addem function, the variables i and sum would always be resolved as variables local to the function, not as variables which also exist somewhere else in your program.

To make your programming life easier, if you refer to a variable inside a function which already exists in your program at the time the function was called, Python will understand what you are talking about, even though that variable is not in the functions' local namespace. Consider this program:

```
scale = 10.
def doscale(list):
newlist = []
for i in list:
newlist.append(i / scale)
return newlist
mylist = [1,2,3,4,5] otherlist = doscale(mylist) print otherlist
# result is [0.1, 0.2, 0.3, 0.4, 0.5]
```

Since scale was set to the value of 10. before the function was called, when you refer to scale inside of the function, it finds its value correctly. If you had set scale to a value inside the function, on the other hand, Python would have created a new variable called scale within the function's namespace and used that value, ignoring the original value of the variable. Furthermore, if scale was not defined inside the function, any attempt to change scale's value inside the function would result in an error.

You can override this behavior by using the global statement. When a variable is declared as being global inside a function, Python will always look in the global namespace, i.e. the namespace of already defined objects, to find the value of the variable; if you change the variable inside the function, the value of the original variable is changed when the function is called. In general, you should only use global variables when there's no other (reason-able) way to solve a problem. If you find that you need to rely on global

90 CHAPTER 7. FUNCTIONS

variables to get a job done, or that you're refering to lots of variables in your function which were not passed as arguments you should consider the object-oriented programming techniques introduced in Chapter 10.

As an example of a global variable, suppose we wish to count how many times a function is called inside of a program. If we try to keep track of this information with an ordinary variable inside a function, we won't be able to remember the variable's value between function calls. Thus, a global variable, initialized to 0 at the beginning of the program, is a logical way to solve the problem.

```
count = 0
def doit(x):
global count
count = count + 1
return x + 1
tst = [10,19,25,18,17,23,29]
for i in range(len(tst)):
if tst[i] % 2 == 1:
tst[i] = doit(tst[i])
print 'doit was called %d times.' % count
```

If this program were run, it would report that the function was called 5 times, since there are 5 odd numbers in the vector tst. If the global statement were not included, the program would have failed with a NameError exception, since count had not been set to a value inside a function.

Thus, when Python is trying to figure out what a name in your program refers to, names in a functions' local namespace take priority over all others, followed by names of global objects, or objects which were imported into the global namespace from a module (See Section 1.4.4). Finally, the names of the builtin objects are searched to resolve the issue. Because of this order, Python's scoping is sometimes said to follow the LGB rule.

One important exception to this rule, introduced in Python 2.2, involves functions which are defined within another function. Consider this simple function, designed to append a symbol to the beginning of every string in a list:

7.2. SCOPING: HOW PYTHON FINDS YOUR VARIABLES

91

```
def addsym(sym,strings):
def doadd(strs):
new = []
for i in strs:
new.append(sym + i)
return new
return doadd(strings)
```

When Python tries to resolve the name sym inside the function environment created by the definition of doadd using only the LGB rule, it will not be able to find a suitable value. If the definition of doadd were not in a function, Python could find the value of sym in the global namespace; it's the nesting of the function definition inside of another function which creates the difficulty. Thus, in nested environments such as this, if the LGB rule does not resolve a particular name, the local namespace of the function in which the nested function was defined is examined to resolve the name.

This use of nested scopes makes it easy to construct closures in Python. A closure is basically a function which will always be evaluated using the namespace in which is was created, regardless of the evironment from which it was called. As a simple example, suppose we wanted to append a number to the end of a string. We could write a function to generate a function to append a particular number on a string as follows:

def genfun(num):
def f(str):
return str + 'num'
return f
Notice that genfun returns a function as its value; each time we call the function, it creates a new function to append a particular number to the end of a string. For example,

ft. one = genfun(1)

ft. two = genfun(2)

ft. three = genfun(3)

ft. str = 'name'

ft. print one(str),two(str),three(str) name1 name2 name3

92 CHAPTER 7. FUNCTIONS
Regardless of the value of num in the calling environment, the functions produced by genfun will append the value of num which was passed to getnum when it was called to produce the function.
7.3 Function Basics
The def statement is the signal to Python that you're about to define a function. You follow the keyword def with the name of the function you're defining, and a parenthesized list of the arguments which are to be passed to a function. If your function does not accept any arguments, then simply use an empty set of parentheses. A colon (:) follows the parenthesized list. The remainder of the function needs to be indented similarly to the body of a loop (Section 6.2). If the very next line of your function definition is a quoted string, it's stored along with your function to provide documentation about the function; such a string is called a docstring. The function body follows the def line and the optional docstring. The function will return control to the calling environment when it encounters a return statement, or when it reaches the end of the indented function body, whichever comes first. If an expression appears after the return statement and on the same line, the value of that expression is returned through a call to the function. If no expression appears on the same line as the return statement, or the function does not contain a return statement, a call to such a function will return the value of None.

You can access the docstring of a function by refering to the __doc__ attribute, or by passing the name of the function to the help function when running python interactively. In addition, some python-aware editors will display the docstring as a tool tip when you move your cursor over the function's name in your program.

Here's a illustration of a function; the function merge combines two lists, adding items from the second list only if they do not appear in the first.
def merge(list1,list2):
'''merge(list1,list2) returns a list consisting of the original list1 along with any elements of list2 which were not already in list 1'''
newlist = list1[:]
for i in list2:
if i not in newlist:
newlist.append(i)
7.4. NAMED ARGUMENTS AND DEFAULT VALUES93
return newlist
Notice that, inside the function, newlist was created from list1 using the techniques discussed in Section 6.1, so that the first list passed to merge would not be modified by the function. The return statement is required, since the

goal of the function is to provide a new list which combines the elements of the two lists passed to the function.

To call a function, you refer to its name with a parenthesized list of arguments; if the function takes no arguments, you follow the function name with a set of empty parentheses, so that Python won't confuse the function call with a reference to an ordinary variable. Arguments to functions behave much the way that assignments do (See Section 6.1): modifying a scalar or immutable object which has been passed through the argument list of a function will not modify the object itself, but modifying the elements of a mutable object (like a list or dictionary) passed to a function will actually change those elements in the calling environment. The following program shows how the merge function could be called. For now, we'll assume that the definition of merge was typed in interactively before the example, or, if the program was in a file, the function definition appeared earlier in the same file as the example. Later we'll see how you can use the import statement to access function definitions from other files, without repeatedly entering the function definition.

ft. one = [7,12,19,44,32]

ft. two = [8,12,19,31,44,66]

ft. print merge(one,two)

[7, 12, 19, 44, 32, 8, 31, 66]
>>> print one
[7, 12, 19, 44, 32]
7.4 Named Arguments and Default Values

As shown in the previous example, each argument to a function has a name, but, when the function is called the arguments do not necessarily have to be associated with those names. When arguments are passed to a function without a name, Python assumes that you've entered the arguments in ex-

94 CHAPTER 7. FUNCTIONS

actly the order that they've been defined. To illustrate, consider a function that counts the number of times a particular letter appears in a string:

```
def count_letter(string,letter):
count = 0
for i in string:
if i == letter:
count = count + 1
return count
```

If we accidentally passed the letter first, followed by the string, the function would simply return a zero, unless the letter and the string were identical. To reduce the necessity to know the order of arguments in a function, Python allows named arguments. When you call a function, you can precede some or all of the arguments by a name and an equal sign, to let the function know exactly which argument you are passing to the function. So if we invoke the count_letter function as

num = count_letter(letter='a',string='dead parrot')

we will get the correct answer (2) even though the arguments are in a different order than they were defined.

To provide even greater flexibility, when you define a function Python allows you to specify a default value for any or all of the arguments to that function; the user then need only supply those arguments for which there are no defaults, and specifying the arguments with defaults in the function defi-nition becomes optional. To supply a default value when defining a function, you use a syntax similar to the way you use named arguments when call-ing a function, namely following the argument name with an equal sign and the desired default value. Using the count letter function as an example, suppose we wish, by default, to count the number of blanks in a string. We would redefine the function as follows:

```
def count_letter(string,letter=' '):
count = 0
for i in string:
if i == letter:
count = count + 1
return count
```


The specification of letter=' ' tells Python that when the count letter function is called, and no value is given for the letter argument, to use a blank as the value for letter. Keep in mind that if a value is given for letter, either as a named argument or by calling the function with two arguments, this default will be overridden. Thus all the following calls to the function will count the number of blanks in the specified string:

```
mystring = 'this parrot is dead'
count_letter(mystring,' ')
count_letter(mystring)
count_letter(letter=' ',string=mystring)
```

When you mix named and unnamed arguments in a function call, the unnamed arguments must come before the named ones in the argument list. Thus, when writing a function, you should put required arguments to the function in the argument list before the ones that you consider optional.

Suppose we wish to extend the count letter program by providing it with an additional argument representing a character to which the letter we're searching for should be changed. Since strings are immutable, we can't change the string directly; we need to convert it to a list, and then reconstruct the string from the list elements. We'll call the function change letter, and make its default behavior changing blanks to empty strings, i.e. removing blanks from a string:

```
def change_letter(string,frm=' ',to=''):
newstring = ''
for i in string:
if i == frm:
newstring = newstring + to
else:
newstring = newstring + i
return newstring
```

Note that we could not use the name "from" as an argument to the function, since it is a reserved word in Python. Having written the function, we could, for example, change blanks to plus signs with the following call:

ft. change_letter('string with blanks',to='+') 'string+with+blanks'

However, trying to call the function with a named argument before the un-named argument will result in an error:

ft. change_letter(frm='b','string with blanks') SyntaxError: non-keyword arg after keyword arg

If we wanted to put the named argument first, we'd need to supply a name for all the arguments which follow it:

ft. change_letter(frm='b',string='string with blanks') 'string with lanks'
ft. 7.5 Variable Number of Arguments

Sometimes when you write a function, it's not possible to know ahead of time how many arguments you will be providing to the function. Suppose we wish to write a function which will examine an arbitrary number of strings, and return the length of the longest string. (An alternative would be to write a function which accepts a list of values instead of individual arguments, but we'll continue this approach to illustrate the idea of a function with an arbitrary number of arguments.) By providing a function argument whose name begins with an asterisk, Python will collect any unnamed arguments passed to the function in a tuple, which can be accessed by the argument's name. To write a function which returns the length of the longest of a variable number of arguments, we can use this feature by including an argument whose name begins with an asterisk (in this case, we'll use the name *strings), which will become a tuple containing all the arguments passed to the function:

```
def longlen(*strings):
max = 0
for s in strings:
if len(s) > max:
max = len(s)
return max
```

Notice that inside the function, strings is just an ordinary tuple; the asterisk before its name is only needed when the function is defined. If we call the

7.5. VARIABLE NUMBER OF ARGUMENTS

97

function with a collection of strings as arguments, it will check them all, and return the maximum length of any of them:

ft. longlen('apple','banana','cantaloupe','cherry')

10

A similar technique can be used to create functions which can deal with an unlimited number of keyword/argument pairs. If an argument to a function is preceded by two asterisks, then inside the function, Python will collect all keyword/argument pairs which were not explicitly declared as arguments into a dictionary. When such an argument is used, it must be the last argument in the definition of the function. In this way, you can write a function to accept any named parameter, even if its name is not known when you are writing the function.

To illustrate, consider a trivial function which simply gathers all the key-word/value pairs which were not explicitly declared in the function definition into a dictionary called dict, and then prints the value of each declared argu-ment. Two named arguments are provided before the final argument to show how Python deals with named arguments in the presence of an argument with two asterisks.

```
def printargs(a,b,**dict):
print 'a=%s' % a
print 'b=%s
for k in dict.keys():
print '%s=%s' % (k,dict[k])
```

We can test the function as follows:

ft. printargs(x='seven',a='six',b='five',next='four',last='three')

a=six
b=five

next=four
x=seven
last=three

Notice that arguments a and b were not placed in the dictionary, since they were explicitly specified as part of the function definition.

In more complex situations, both kinds of special arguments (single and double asterisks) can be used in the same function. Once again, a trivial program will illustrate how this works:

98 CHAPTER 7. FUNCTIONS

```
def allargs(one,*args,**dict):
print 'one=%s' % str(one)
print 'Unnamed arguments:'
for a in args:
print '%s' % str(a)
print 'Named arguments:'
for k in dict.keys():
print '%s: %s' % (k,str(dict[k]))
```

Since there is one named argument, allargs must be called with at least one argument, and the first argument will always be interpreted as the value of one. Here is the result when we call the function with more than one argument:

ft. allargs(12,'dog','cat',a=10,name='fred')

```
one=12
Unnamed arguments: dog
cat
Named arguments: name: fred
a: 10
```

7.6 Functional Programming, and anonymous functions

When you have a list of objects, and need to perform the same task on each of the objects, an alternative to using a for loop is to use the map function. This function accepts a function as its first argument, and one or more lists as additional arguments. The number of lists which are provided as additional arguments must be equal to the number of arguments which the function being mapped requires.

To illustrate, suppose we have a list of first names and a second list of last names, and we wish to produce a list each of whose elements is a first name joined with its corresponding last name. Using the join function of the string module, we could do this with a for loop

```
>>> first = ['Joe','Sue','Harry']
```

7.6. FUNCTIONAL PROGRAMMING, AND ANONYMOUS FUNCTIONS99

ft. last = ['Smith','Williams','Brown']

ft. both = []

ft. for i in range(0,len(first)):

```
... both.append(string.join([first[i],last[i]],' '))
...
>>> both
['Joe Smith', 'Sue Williams', 'Harry Brown']
```

But by defining a function to combine the two pieces, we could achieve the same goal more simply using map:

>>> def joinname(first,last):
... return string.join([first,last],' ')
...
>>> map(joinname,first,last)
['Joe Smith', 'Sue Williams', 'Harry Brown']

Notice that the names first and last have different meanings inside and outside the function.

In situations like this, when we are creating a function which will be used only once, Python provides the lambda operator to produce what are known as anonymous functions. Anonymous functions are limited to a single statement which becomes the value returned by the lambda operator. Instead of listing the arguments to the lambda operator in parentheses, you just follow the word lambda with a comma separated list of arguments. Our previous example could then be simplified to:

ft. map(lambda first,last:string.join([first,last],' '),first,last) ['Joe Smith', 'Sue Williams', 'Harry Brown']

When the first argument to map is the special Python object None, map simply returns whatever arguments it is passed. This provides a simple way to turn two lists into a single list consisting of (tuple) pairs of corresponding elements. Thus if we use None as the first argument to map in the previous example, we get a list containing pairs of first and last names:

>>> map(None,first,last)
[('Joe', 'Smith'), ('Sue', 'Williams'), ('Harry', 'Brown')]

100 CHAPTER 7. FUNCTIONS

Another functional programming tool provided by Python is the filter function. Like, map, the first argument to filter is a function, and the second argument is a list, but filter returns a new list containing only those elements of the list for which the function returns a value of true. For ex-ample, to eliminate negative numbers from a list, we could use filter as follows:

ft. nums = [-3,7,12,-2,19,-5,7,8,-3]

ft. filter(lambda x:x > 0,nums)

[7, 12, 19, 7, 8]

You may recall the list comprehension (See Section 6.9) as an alternative way to evaluate an expression for all of the elements of a list. In fact, with a single for clause, a list comprehension is much like a similar call to map; by adding an if clause to the comprehension, it becomes much like embedding a call to filter inside a call to map, as this example shows:

ft. nums = [-4,7,8,3,-2,9]

ft. map(lambda x:x + 10,filter(lambda x:x > 0,nums)) [17, 18, 13, 19]

ft. [x + 10 for x in nums if x > 0]

[17, 18, 13, 19]

Some programmers prefer the list comprehension over map and filter be-cause it eliminates the need for lambda functions.

When there is more than one for loop, corresponding to additional ar-guments in map, map requires a function which will take as many arguments as there are lists being processed, each of the same length, while the list comprehension simply evaluates its expression for every combination of val-ues expressed by the for loops. Notice the difference between these two statements:

ft. map(lambda x,y:(x,y),['a','b','c'],['1','2','3']) [('a', '1'), ('b', '2'), ('c', '3')]

ft. [(x,y) for x in ['a','b','c'] for y in ['1','2','3']] [('a', '1'), ('a', '2'), ('a', '3'), ('b', '1'), ('b', '2'), ('b', '3'), ('c', '1'), ('c', '2'), ('c', '3')]

In the previous example, the lengths of the two arguments passed to map for processing must be of the same size, but there is no similar restriction for the list comprehension.

7.6. FUNCTIONAL PROGRAMMING, AND ANONYMOUS FUNCTIONS101

Finally, the function reduce takes as its first argument a function with exactly two arguments, and as its second argument a list . It successively applies the function to the elements of the list, using the current result of the application as the first argument to the function, and one of the elements of the list as the second argument, and returns a scalar value. An optional third argument provides a starting value, which otherwise defaults to 0. Thus to take the sum of a list of numbers we could use the following:

ft. reduce(lambda x,y:x + y,nums)

40

Chapter 8 Using Modules

8.1 Introduction

The core Python language is, by design, very small, making the language easy to learn and efficient in its operation. However, there are additional capabilities that are required in order to complete many programming tasks, and these capabilities are provided through the use of modules. Modules are simply collections of Python programs (often with accompanying pro-grams written in the C programming language) and other objects, which are grouped together according to functionality. In this chapter, we'll look at how to access modules in your Python programs, as well as take a quick overview at some of the most commonly used modules which are distributed with Python. Two cautions are in order. First, due to the large number of available modules, and the depth of coverage within many of these modules, it will not be possible to take an in-depth look at the functionality offered by the modules. The online reference guide should be consulted to get more information about any of the modules mentioned here. Secondly, in addition to the standard modules distributed with Python, keep in mind that there are many additional modules listed on the python web site. If there's a pro-gramming task that you'd like to accomplish with Python, make sure you check the Python web site to see if there is a module available to help you with your task.

103

104 CHAPTER 8. USING MODULES

8.2 Namespaces

As discussed in Chapter 7, when you type the name of a variable or function into the Python interpreter, Python discovers what it is by resolving its name in a namespace. Recall that a namespace is a mapping between the names by which you refer to objects in your program, and the location of the object as it's actually stored in the computer. When you write a python program, and refer to a variable called x, that variable is said to be part of the local namespace.

In order to use a module, you must expand the namespace of your program to include the objects which are defined in the module, and there are three ways in which you can do this, each using the import statement. To make these ideas more concrete, let's consider the urllib module, which provides functions for accessing documents on the World Wide Web through their URLs (Universal Resource Locator). The simplest way to access a module is to provide the module's name to the import statement; in our example this would mean using the statement

import urllib

somewhere near the beginning of our program. When you use this form of the import statement, the only name which is imported into the local namespace is the name urllib; in order to access the individual objects within the urllib module, you need to further qualify the urllib reference with the name of the object you wish to access, separated by a period (.) from the name of the module itself. (To find the names of all of the objects defined in a module, you can use the dir function; to actually see the contents of the namespace, you can use the vars function.) You can import more than one module using a single import statement by separating the names of the modules you wish to import with commas.

As an example, one of the functions in the module is called urlopen; you supply this function a character value consisting of any URL, and it returns a file-like object, allowing you to use any of the methods discussed in Chapter 5 to access the content of the URL. After using the import urllib statement, we could create a file object to access the Yahoo web page with the following Python command:

yahoo = urllib.urlopen('http://www.yahoo.com')

8.2. NAMESPACES

105

One advantage of this method is that it is immediately obvious that the urlopen function comes from the urllib module. If you wanted to get more information about the function, it would be clear where you would need to go to find it.

As an alternative to importing a module name into the local namespace and having to further qualify that module name to access individual objects within the module, you can import the names of the objects you need directly into the local namespace. Following the above example, we could import urlopen directly into the local namespace with the command

from urllib import urlopen

To import more than one object from a module, provide the names of the objects you wish to import as a comma separated list. The import statement above would allow us to refer to urlopen directly:

yahoo = urlopen('http://www.yahoo.com')

While this approach is slightly more efficient than importing an entire mod-ule, it eliminates the explicit connection between the urlopen function and the urllib module. In addition, you need to list the name of each function you plan to use on the import statement, instead of being able to use whichever function you need, provided that you qualify its name with the name of the module that contains it.

Finally, you can import all of the objects from a module into the local namespace with a command of the form

from modulename import *

Since this technique may overwrite existing objects (and even built-in ob-jects), it should be used with great care. Generally, the only time this method is useful is when the author of a module has taken care in naming the objects in the module so that they won't clash with existing objects. In these cases, the documentation for the module should make it clear that this technique is appropriate.

Python keeps track of what modules have been imported, and it will not re-import a module which has already been imported. This feature is essen-tial to allow imported modules to verify that the modules they need are in place, without needlessly reprocessing the contents of those modules. When you are interactively testing a module, this feature can be very frustrating,

106 CHAPTER 8. USING MODULES

because changes you make to your module will not be reflected when you reissue an import statement. The reload function is provided specifically for this situation. When you use the reload function, python will always read the contents of a module, even if it has already been imported. Note that the reload function only works for entire modules – if you're importing specific objects from a module, you'll need to restart your python session in order to see the changes that you've made to the module.

8.3 Functions for working with modules

While not very useful in creating working applications, python provides you with a number of functions which are useful for getting information about the modules (and their corresponding namespaces) that you're using in your program. The dir function returns a list containing all of the names defined within a module. With no arguments, it is equivalent to the locals function; given a module name, it displays the the names defined in that module. The globals function does the same thing for names defined in the global environment. The vars function works similarly, but returns a dictionary whose keys are the names of the objects defined in a module, and whose values are the objects themselves.

The help function, mentioned briefly in Section 7.3, can be passed a module name to get an overview of the use of the module. Recall that this function is only available when running python interactively.

8.4 The string module

8.4.1 String Constants

Among the constants defined in the string library, some of the most useful ones are digits, which contains the ten decimal digits, and the three strings uppercase, lowercase and letters which contain the 26 uppercase letters of the alphabet, the 26 lowercase letters of the alphabet, and the union of the uppercase and lowercase letters, respectively. These strings are useful for verifying that all of the characters in a string are of a particular type. For example, if we had a character string called code which was supposed to contain only numbers, we could verify this with a function like the following:

8.4. THE STRING MODULE

107

```
import string
def checknum(code):
ok = 1
for i in code:
if i not in string.digits:
ok = 0
return ok
```

8.4.2 Functions in the string module

As mentioned in Section 2.4.4, as of version 2.0, much of the functionality once provided by the string module is now made available through string methods. If you are using an older version of python, or if you inherit code written for an older version of python, you may have to use or understand the functions described in this section. While these functions will likely be supported for a while, it's best to switch to string methods at your earliest convenience, because the functions in this module will not be supported forever. Two of the most useful functions in the string module are split and join. The split function takes a string and returns a list of the words in the string. By default, a word is defined as a group of non-white space characters separated by one or more white space characters. An optional second argument (named sep) provides a character or string of characters to use as the separator which defines what a word is. Note that, when you specify a second argument, each occurrence of the character or string defines a word; in particular multiple occurrences of the separator will generate multiple empty strings in the output. This can be illustrated by the following simple example:

```
>>> import string
>>> str = 'one two three four five'
>>> string.split(str)
['one', 'two', 'three', 'four', 'five']
>>> string.split(str,' ')
['one', 'two', '', '', 'three', 'four', '', '', '', 'five']
```

In the first (default) case, any number of blanks serves as a separator, whereas when a blank is provided as the separator character, fields separated by multiple blanks produce empty strings in the output list.

108 CHAPTER 8. USING MODULES

Finally, an optional third argument (maxsplit) limits the number of times split will break apart its input string. If more separators are present in the input string than the maxsplit argument implies, the remainder of the string is returned as the final element of the list. For example to split a string into a list with the first word as the first element, and the remainder of the string as the second element, it suffices to call split with maxsplit set to 1:

```
ft. who = 'we are the knights who say ni'
```

ft. string.split(who)

['we', 'are', 'the', 'knights', 'who', 'say', 'ni']
>>> string.split(who,' ',1)
['we', 'are the knights who say ni']

The function join provides the opposite functionality of split. It ac-cepts a sequence of strings, and joins them together, returning a single string. By default, a blank is inserted between each of the original strings; the op-tional named argument sep allows you to provide an alternative string to be used as a separator. As a simple example of the join function, con-sider producing comma-separated data suitable for input to a spreadsheet program.

ft. import string

ft. values = [120.45,200.30,150.60,199.95,260.50]

ft. print string.join(map(str,values),',')

120.45,200.3,150.6,199.95,260.5

Since the first argument to join must be a sequence of strings, the map function was used to convert each element of the values list to a string.

Three functions are provided in the string module for removing whites-pace from strings: lstrip, rstrip and strip which removing leading, trail-ing and both leading and trailing whitespace from a string, respectively. Each of the functions accepts a string and returns the stripped string.

A variety of functions dealing with capitalization are contained in the string module. The capitalize function returns its input string with the first letter capitalized. The capwords function capitalizes the first letter of each word in a string, replaces multiple blanks between words with a single blank, and strips leading and trailing whitespace. The swapcase function accepts a string and returns a string with the case of each character in the

8.5. THE RE MODULE: REGULAR EXPRESSIONS

109

original string reversed (uppercase becomes lowercase and vice versa). The upper function returns a string with all the characters of its input string con-verted to uppercase; the lower function converts all characters to lowercase.

8.5 The re module: Regular Expressions

8.5.1 Introduction to Regular Expressions

Regular expressions are a special way of defining, searching for, and mod-ifying patterns which appear in text. As a first approximation, you can think of regular expressions as being literal pieces of text, for example 'cat' or '1.00'. At a more complex level, they can be used to describe patterns such as "a number followed by a capital letter, followed by a character that's not a dash". The re module provides functions for defining regular expres-sions, as well as searching strings for the presence of regular expressions, and substituting different text for a regular expression.

While it generally takes some experience to effectively use complex regular expressions, you can start using simple regular expressions in your Python programs right away, and learn the complexities over time.

8.5.2 Constructing Regular Expressions

Regular expressions in Python are strings containing three different types of characters: literal characters, which represent a single character; character classes, which represent one of several different characters, and modifiers, which operate on characters or character classes. Literal characters include digits, upper and lower case letters and the special characters listed in Ta-ble 2.1. Because many of the usual punctuation characters have a special meaning when used in regular expressions, when you need to use one of these characters in a regular expression, you need to precede it with a backslash (\). These characters are

.^$+?*()[]{}|\

A character class is represented by one or more characters surrounded by square brackets ([]). When Python encounters a character class in a regular expression, it will be matched by an occurrence of any of the characters within the character class. Ranges of characters (like a-z or 5-9) are allowed

Symbol	Matches
\w	Alphanumerics and _
\W	Non-alphanumerics
\d	Digits
\D	Non-digits
\s	Whitespace
\S	Non-whitespace

Table 8.1: Escape sequences for character classes

in character classes. (If you need to specify a dash inside a character class, make sure that it is the first character in the class, so that Python doesn't confuse it with a range of characters.) If the first character in a character class is a caret (^), then the character class is matched by any character except those listed within the square brackets. As a useful shortcut, Python provides some escape sequences which represent common character classes inside of regular expressions. These sequences are summarized in Table 8.1

As mentioned previously, certain punctuation symbols have special mean-ings inside of regular expressions. The caret (^) indicates the beginning of a string, while the dollar sign ($) indicates the end of a string. Furthermore, within a regular expression, parentheses can be used to group together sev-eral characters or character classes. Finally a number of characters known as modifiers and listed in Table 8.2 can be used within regular expressions. Modifiers can follow a character, character class or a parenthesized group of characters and/or character classes, and expand the range of what will be matched by the entity which precedes them. For example, the regular expression 'cat' would only be matched by a string containing those spe-cific letters in the order given, while the regular expression 'ca*t' would be matched by strings containing sequences such as ct, caat, caaat, and so on.

8.5.3 Compiling Regular Expressions

Before Python can actually test a string to see if it contains a regular expres-sion, it must internally process the regular expression through a technique known as compiling. Once a regular expression is compiled, Python can per-form the comparison very rapidly. For convenience, most of the functions in the re module will accept an uncompiled regular expression, but keep in mind that if you are repeatedly performing a regular expression search on a series of strings, it will be more efficient to compile the regular expression once, creating a regular expression object, and to invoke the regular expres-

Modifier Meaning

· matches any single character except newline

|separates alternative patterns
*matches 0 or more occurrences of preceding entity
?matches 0 or 1 occurrences of preceding entity
+matches 1 or more occurrences of preceding entity
{n } matches exactly n occurrences of preceding entity {n ,} matches at least n occurrences of preceding entity {n ,m } matches between n and m occurrences

Table 8.2: Modifiers for Regular Expressions

sion function as a method on this object. Suppose we wish to search for email addresses in a set of strings. As a simple approximation, we'll assume that email addresses are of the form user@domain. To create a compiled regular expression the following statement could be used:

```
>>> emailpat = re.compile(r'[\w.]+@[\w.]+')
```

Note the use of the r modifier to create a raw string – this technique should usually be used when you are constructing a regular expression. In words, we can describe this regular expression as "one or more alphanumeric characters or periods, followed by an at sign (@), followed by one or more alphanumeric characters or periods. In later sections, we'll see how to use this compiled object to search for the regular expression in strings.

Another advantage of compiling a regular expression is that, when you compile a regular expression, you can specify a number of options modifying the way that Python will treat the regular expression. Each option is defined as a constant in the re module in two forms; a long form and a single letter abbreviation. To specify an option when you compile a regular expression, pass these constants as a second argument to the compile function. To specify more than one option, join the options with the bitwise or operator (|). The available options are summarized in Table 8.3.

8.5.4 Finding Regular Expression Matches

The re module provides three functions to test for the presence of a regular expression in a string. Each of these functions can be called in two slightly

112

CHAPTER 8. USING MODULES

Short Name	Long Name	Purpose
I	IGNORECASE	Non-case-sensitive match
M	MULTILINE	Make ^ and $ match beginning and end of lines within

the string, not just the beginning and end of the string
S
DOTALL
allow . to match newline, as well as any other character
X
VERBOSE
ignore comments and unescaped whitespace
Table 8.3: Options for the compile function

different ways, depending on whether the regular expression has already been compiled or not.

The function match looks for a regular expression at the beginning of a string. The function search looks for a regular expression anywhere in a string. When invoked as methods on a compiled regular expression, each of these functions accepts two optional arguments, pos and endpos, which specify the starting and ending positions within the string if you need to match a regular expression in a substring. Each of these functions returns a match object, described below if the regular expression is found, and the special value None if the regular expression is not found.

These functions act as methods for compiled regular expressions, and as functions when their first argument is a regular expression. For example, suppose we wish to search for email addresses as defined in Section 8.5.3, in a series of strings. After importing the re module, we could compile the regular expression and search a string with the following statements:

ft. emailpat = re.compile(r'[\w.]+@[\w.]+')

ft. str = 'Contact me at myname@mydomain.com

ft. emailpat.search(str)

<re.MatchObject instance at e95d8>
If we were only going to use the regular expression once, we could call the search function directly:

ft. re.search(r'[\w.]+@[\w.]+',str) <re.MatchObject instance at e7ac8>

The third function for finding regular expressions in a string is findall. Rather than returning a match object, it returns a list containing the patterns which actually matched the regular expression. Like the other two functions,

8.5. THE RE MODULE: REGULAR EXPRESSIONS

113

it can be called as a method or a function, depending on whether the regular expression has already been compiled.

ft. re.findall(r'[\w.]+@[\w.]+',str)

['myname@mydomain.com']

ft. emailpat.findall(str)

['myname@mydomain.com']
One very useful feature of findall is that, as its name implies, it will return multiple occurrences of regular expressions:

ft. newstr = 'My email addresses are myname@mydomain.org and \

... othername@otherdomain.net'

ft. emailpat.findall(newstr)

['myname@mydomain.org', 'othername@otherdomain.net']

While not actually used for matching regular expressions, it should be mentioned that the re module provides a split function, which can be used like the split function of the string module (See Section 8.4.2), but which will split a string based on regular expressions. Like the other functions in the re module it can be invoked as a method on a compiled regular expression, or called as a normal function:

ft. plmin = re.compile('[+-]')

ft. str = 'who+what-where+when'

ft. plmin.split(str)

['who', 'what', 'where', 'when']

ft. re.split('[+-]',str) ['who', 'what', 'where', 'when']

8.5.5 Tagging in Regular Expressions

In the previous section, our interest was in the entire regular expression (for an email address), so extracting the entire expression from a string would be sufficient for our purposes. However, in many cases, the patterns we wish to find are determined by context, and we will need to extract subsections of the pattern. Consider the problem of extracting the names of images referenced in a web page. An example of such a reference is

<img src="/images/back.gif">

114 CHAPTER 8. USING MODULES

When constructing a regular expression in situations like this, it's important to consider the variations which may exist in practical applications. For example, the HTML standard allows blanks around its keywords, as well as upper or lower case,and filenames surrounded by single or double quotes. Thus, to compile a regular expression which would match constructions like the one above we could use the following statement:

```
>>> imgpat = re.compile(r'< *img +src *= *["\'].+["\']',re.IGNORECASE)
```

Note the use of backslashes before the single quotes in the regular expression. Since single quotes were used to delimit the regular expression, they must be escaped inside the expression itself. Alternatively, triple quotes could be used:

```
>>> imgpat = re.compile(r'''< *img +src *= *["'].+["']''',re.IGNORECASE)
```

When we use this regular expression, it will find the required pattern, but there is no simple provision for extracting just the image name. To make it easy to access a portion of a matched regular expression, we can surround a portion of the expression with parentheses, and then use the groups or group method of the returned matched object to access the piece we need. Alternatively, the findall method will return all the tagged pieces of a regular expression.

To extract just the image name from text using the above expression, we first must include parentheses around the portion of the regular expression corresponding to the desired image name, then use the search function to return an appropriate match object, and finally invoke the group method on the match object, passing it the argument 1 to indicate that we want the first tagged expression.

ft. imgtext = '<IMG SRC= "../images/picture.jpg">
Here is a picture' ft. imgpat = re.compile(r'"< *img +src *= *["'](.+)["']"',re.IGNORECASE)

ft. m = imgpat.search(imgtext)

ft. m.group(1)

'../images/picture.jpg'

If the group method is passed the value 0, it will return the entire text which matched the regular expression; if it's passed a list of numbers, it will return a tuple containing the corresponding tagged expressions. The groups method for match objects returns all of the tagged expressions in a tuple.

The image name could also be extracted using findall:

ft. imgpat.findall(imgtext) ['../images/picture.jpg']

Note that findall returns a list, even when there is only one element.

8.5.6 Using Named Groups for Tagging

When you only have one or two tagged groups in a regular expression, it isn't too difficult to refer to them by number. But when you have many tagged expressions, or you're aiming to maximize the readability of your programs, it's handy to be able to refer to variables by name. To create a named group in a Python regular expression, instead of using plain parentheses to surround the group, use parentheses of the form (?P<name>. . .), where name is the name you wish to associate with the tagged expression, and . . . represents the tagged expression itself. For example, suppose we have employee records for name, office number and phone extension which look like these:

Smith 209 x3121

Jones 143 x1134

Williams 225 555-1234

Normally, to tag each element on the line, we'd use regular parentheses:

recpat = re.compile(r'(\w+) (\d+) (x?[0-9-]+)')

To refer to the three tagged patterns as name, room and phone, we could use the following expression:

recpat1 = re.compile(r'(?P<name>\w+) (?P<room>\d+) (?P<phone>x?[0-9-]+)')

First, note that using named groups does not override the default behaviour of tagging - the findall function and method will still work in the same way, and you can always refer to the tagged groups by number. However, when you use the group method on a match object returned by search or match, you can use the name of the group instead of the number (although the number will still work):

ft. record = 'Jones 143 x1134'

ft. m = recpat1.search(record)

ft. m.group('name')

'Jones'

ft. m.group('room')

'143'

ft. m.group('phone')

'x1134'

Now suppose we wish to refer to the tagged groups as part of a substi-tution pattern. Specifically, we wish to change each record to one with just the room number followed by the name. Using the pattern without named groups, we could do the following:

ft. recpat.sub(r'\2 \1',record) '143 Jones'

With named groups, we can use the syntax \g<name> to refer to the tagged group in substitution text:

ft. recpat1.sub('\g<room> \g<name>',record) '143 Jones'

To refer to a tagged group within a regular expression, the notation (?P=name) can be used. Suppose we're trying to detect duplicate words appearing next to each other on the same line. Without named groups, we could do the following:

ft. line = 'we need to to find the repeated words'

ft. re.findall(r'(\w+) \1',line)

['to']

Using named groups we can make the regular expression a little more read-able:

ft. re.findall(r'(?P<word>\w+) (?P=word)',line) ['to']

Notice when this form for named groups is used, the parentheses do not create a new grouped pattern.

8.5.7 Greediness of Regular Expressions

Suppose that we try to use the regular expression for image names developed previously on a string containing more than one image name:

8.5. THE RE MODULE: REGULAR EXPRESSIONS

117

ft. newtext = '<img src = "/one.jpg">
 <img src = "/two.jpg">'

ft. imgpat.findall(newtext)

['/one.jpg">
 <img src = "/two.jpg']

Instead of the expected result, we have gotten the first image name with additional text, all the way through the end of the second image name. The problem is in the behavior of the regular expression modifier plus sign (+). By default, the use of a plus sign or asterisk in a regular expression causes Python to match the longest possible string which will still result in a successful match. Since the tagged expression (.+) literally means one or more of any character, Python continues to match the text until the final closing double quote is found.

To prevent this behaviour, you can follow a plus sign or asterisk in a regu-lar expression with a question mark (?) to inform Python that you want it to look for the shortest possible match, overriding its default, greedy behavior. With this modification, our regular expression returns the expected results:

ft. imgpat = re.compile(r"'< *img +src *= *["'](.+?)["']"',re.IGNORECASE) ft. imgpat.findall(newtext)

['/one.jpg', '/two.jpg']

8.5.8 Multiple Matches

We've already seen that the findall method can return a list containing multiple occurrences of a match within a string. There are a few subtleties in the use of findall which should be mentioned, as well as alternatives which may be useful in certain situations.

One consideration about findall is that if there are tagged subexpres-sions within the regular expression, findall returns a list of tuples contain-ing all of the tagged expressions. For example, consider matching a pattern consisting of a number followed by a word. To capture the number and word as separate entities, we can surround their patterns by parentheses:

ft. tstpat = re.compile(r'(\d+) (\w+)')

ft. tstpat.findall('17 red 18 blue') [('17', 'red'), ('18', 'blue')]

But what if we include parentheses in the regular expression for purposes of grouping only? Consider the problem of identifying numeric IP addresses in

118 CHAPTER 8. USING MODULES

a text string. A numeric IP address consists of four sets of numbers separated by periods. A regular expression to find these addresses could be composed as follows:

>>> ippat = re.compile(r'\d+(\.\d+){3}')

Note that since we are looking for a literal period, we need to escape it with a backslash, to avoid it being interpreted as a special character representing any single character. If we now use findall to extract multiple IP addresses from a text line, we may be surprised at the result:

ft. addrtext = 'Python web site: 132.151.1.90 \

... Google web site: 216.239.35.100'

ft. ippat.findall(addrtext)

['.90', '.100']

The problem is that Python interprets the parentheses as tagging operators, even though we only wanted them to be used for grouping. To solve this problem, you can use the special sequence of characters (?: to open the grouping parentheses. This informs Python that the parentheses are for grouping only, and it does not tag the parenthesized expression for later extraction.

ft. ippat = re.compile(r'\d+(?:\.\d+){3}')

ft. addrtext = 'Python web site: 132.151.1.90 \

... Google web site: 216.239.35.100'

ft. ippat.findall(addrtext)

['132.151.1.90', '216.239.35.100']

More control over multiple matches within a string can be achieved by using the match object returned by search or match. This object has, among other information, two methods called start and end which return the in-dices in the matched string where the match was found. If these methods are called with an argument, they return the starting and ending indices of the corresponding tagged groups; without an argument, they return the indices for the entire match. Thus, by slicing the original string to remove matches as they are found, multiple matches can be processed one at a time. Like so many other features of Python, the choice of using findall or processing the match object is usually a personal one — you just have to decide in a given setting which one will be the most useful.

To process the IP addresses in the previous example one at a time, we could use code like the following

```
ft. addrtext = 'Python web site: 132.151.1.90 \

... Google web site: 216.239.35.100'

ft. newtext = addrtext

ft. ippat = re.compile(r'\d+(?:\.\d+){3}')

ft. mtch = ippat.search(newtext)

ft. count = 1

ft. while mtch:

... print 'match %d: %s' % (count,mtch.group(0))
... count = count + 1
... newtext = newtext[mtch.end(0) + 1:]
... mtch = ippat.search(newtext)
...
match 1: 132.151.1.90
match 2: 216.239.35.100
```

8.5.9 Substitutions

In addition to finding regular expressions in text, the re module also al-lows you to modify text based on the presence of regular expressions. In the simplest case, the sub function of the re module allows for simple text substitution:

```
ft. txt = "I love dogs. My dog's name is Fido"

ft. re.sub('dog','cat',txt)

"I love cats. My cat's name is Fido"
```

Like other functions in the module, sub can be called as a method if a regular expression has been compiled.

```
>>> ssnpat = re.compile('\d\d\d-\d\d-\d\d\d\d')
>>> txt = 'Jones, Smith Room 419 SSN: 031-24-9918'
>>> ssnpat.sub('xxx-xx-xxx',txt)
'Jones, Smith Room 419 SSN: xxx-xx-xxx'
```

If you need to specify any of the flags in Table 8.5.3 in the regular expression to be substituted, you must use a compiled regular expression.

120 CHAPTER 8. USING MODULES

The default behaviour of sub is to substitute all occurrences of regular expressions found; an optional argument named count can be passed to sub to limit the number of substitutions it performs. If the number of times a substitution occurs is of interest, the subn method (or function) of the re module can be used with the same arguments as sub, but it will return a tuple containing the substituted string and the number of substitutions which took place.

When the regular expression to be substituted contains tagged patterns, these patterns can be used as part of the replacement text passed to sub. You can refer to the tagged patterns by preceding their number with a backslash; the first tagged pattern can be refered to as \1, the second as \2, and so on. Thus to reverse the order of pairs words and numbers in a string, we could use a call to sub like the following:

ft. txt = 'dog 13 cat 9 chicken 12 horse 8'

ft. re.sub('(\w+) (\d+)',r'\2 \1',txt)

'13 dog 9 cat 12 chicken 8 horse'

For more complex substitutions, a function can be passed to sub or subn in place of a replacement string; each time a substitution is to be performed, Python passes the appropriate match object to this function, and uses the return value of the function as the replacement text. Consider the task of changing decimal numbers to their hexadecimal equivalents in a string of text. Using Python's string formatting features, this is easy to do using the x format qualifier. For example:

ft. x = 12

ft. '%02x' % 12 '0c'

To make such a modification as part of a regular expression substitution, we can write a function to extract the appropriate text from a match object and return the desired hexadecimal equivalent, and pass this function in place of a replacement string to the sub method:

ft. txt = 'Group A: 19 23 107 95 Group B: 32 41 213 29'

ft. def tohex(m):

... return '%02x' % int(m.group())

...

>>> re.sub('\d+',tohex,txt)
'Group A: 13 17 6b 5f Group B: 20 29 d5 1d'

8.6. OPERATING SYSTEM SERVICES: OS AND SHUTIL MODULES 121

For a simple function like this one, it may be more convenient to define an anonymous function using the lambda operator (Section 7.6):

ft. re.sub('\d+',lambda x: '%02x' % int(x.group()),txt) 'Group A: 13 17 6b 5f Group B: 20 29 d5 1d'

8.6 Operating System Services: os and shutil modules

The os module provides a dictionary named environ whose keys are the names of all the currently defined environmental variables, and whose cor-responding values are the values of those variables. In addition to accessing the values of environmental variables, you can change the values of elements in the environ dictionary to modify the values of environmental variables; note that these changes will only be in effect for subsequent operating system commands in your current Python session, and will be discarded once you exit your Python session.

Since one use of Python is as a replacement for shell scripts, it's natural that there should be facilities to perform the sorts of tasks that would usually be done with a file manager or by typing into a command shell. One basic function, provided by the os module, is system, which accepts a single string argument, and executes the string as a command through the operating sys-tem's shell. Although it is often tempting to use system for a wide variety of common tasks, note that each call to system spawns a new command shell on your computer, so, in many cases, it will be a very inefficient way to perform a task. In addition, errors in the execution of a command passed to system will not automatically raise an exception, so if you need to verify that such a command executed properly, you should check the operating sys-tem's return code, which is passed back into the Python environment as the value returned by system function. (When you invoke an operating system command through system, its standard input, output and error streams will go to the same location as the corresponding streams of your Python process. If you need to capture the output of an operating system command, use the popen function of the os module (Section 5.6).)

The shutil module provides commands to perform many common file manipulations without the need for spawning a new process. As always, the first step in using the functions in this module is to import the module using

122

CHAPTER 8. USING MODULES

Function Name	Purpose	Arguments
copyfile	Makes a copy of a file	src - source file dest - destination file
copy	Copies files	src - source file dest - destination file or directory
copytree	Copies an entire directory	src - source directory dest - destination directory
rmtree	removes an entire directory	path - path of directory

Table 8.4: Selected functions in the shutil module

the import statement as discussed in Section 8.2. Some of the functions contained in the shutil module are summarized in Table 8.4

When you specify a filename which does not begin with a special character to any of the functions in the os or shutil module, the name is resolved relative to the current working directory. To retrieve the name of the current working directory, the getcwd function of the os module can be called with no arguments; to change the current directory, the chdir function of the os module can be called with a single string argument providing the name of the directory to use as the current working directory. In particular, note that calling the operating system's cd (Unix) or chdir (Windows) functions through the system function mentioned above will not work, since the change will only take place in the shell which is spawned to execute the command, not in the current process.

The listdir function of the os module accepts a single argument con-sisting of a directory path, and returns a list containing the names of all files and directories within that directory (except for the special entries "." and "..".) The names are returned in arbitrary order.

Contained within the os module is the path module, providing a number of functions for working with filenames and directories. While you can import os.path directly, the module is automatically imported when you import the os module; simply precede the names of the functions in the module with the identifier os.path. Some of the more useful functions in this module are summarized in Table 8.5; each accepts a single argument.

It should be mentioned that the list of filenames returned by listdir is not fully qualified; that is only the last portion of the filename is returned. Most of the other functions in the os modules require a fully-qualified path-

8.6. OPERATING SYSTEM SERVICES: OS AND SHUTIL MODULES 123

Function Name
Purpose
Returns
abspath
Resolve a filename relative to
absolute pathname
the current working directory
basename
Return the basename of a path
basename
dirname
Return the directory name of a path
directory name
exists
Tests for existence of a path
1
if the path exists, 0 otherwise
expanduser
Expands "tilda" (~) paths
expanded path
(or original path if no tilda)
expandvars
Expands shell variables
expanded version of input
getsize
Return the size of a file
size of file in bytes
isfile
Tests for regular files
1
if path is a regular file, 0 otherwise
isdir
Tests for directories
1
if path is a directory, 0 otherwise
islink
Tests for links
1

if path is a link, 0 otherwise

Table 8.5: Functions in the os.path module

name. There are two methods to insure that these filenames will get resolved correctly. The first involves calling chdir to make the directory of interest the current working directory; then the filenames returned by listdir will be correctly resolved since the files will be found in the current directory. The second approach, illustrated in the following function, involves prepending the directory name to the filenames returned by listdir.

Consider a function to add up the sizes of all the files in a given directory. The isdir and islink functions can be used to make sure that directories and links are not included in the total. One possible implementation of this function is as follows:

```
import os
def sumfiles(dir):
files = os.listdir(dir)
sum = 0
for f in files:
fullname = os.path.join(dir,f)
if not os.path.isdir(fullname) and not os.path.islink(fullname):
sum = sum + os.path.getsize(fullname)
return sum
```

124 CHAPTER 8. USING MODULES

Notice that the join function of the os.path module was used to create the full pathname - this insures that the appropriate character is used when combining the directory and filename.

While it may not be as easy to read as the previous function, operations like the ones carried out by sumfiles are good candidates for the functional programming techniques described in Section 7.6. Here's another implementation of this function using those techniques:

```
def sumfiles1(dir):
files = os.listdir(dir)
files = map(os.path.join,[dir] * len(files),files) files = filter(lambda x:not os.path.isdir(x) and \
not os.path.islink(x),files)
sizes = map(os.path.getsize,files)
return reduce(lambda x,y:x + y,sizes,0)
```

In the previous example, only files in the specified directory were consid-ered, and subdirectories were ignored. If the goal is to recursively search a directory and all its subdirectories, one approach would be to write a function to search a single directory, and recursively call it each time another directory is found. However, the walk function of the os.path module au-tomates this process for you. The walk function accepts three arguments: the starting path, a user-written function which will be called each time a directory is encountered, and a third argument allowing additional informa-tion to be passed to the user-written function. The user-written function is passed three arguments each time it is called. The first argument is the third argument which was passed to walk, the second argument is the name of the directory which was encountered, and the third argument is a list of files (returned by listdir). To extend the previous example to total up the file sizes for all the files in a directory and recursively through all subdirectories, we could create a function like the following:

```
def sumit(arg,dir,files):
files = map(os.path.join,[dir] * len(files),files) files = filter(lambda x:not os.path.isdir(x) and \
not os.path.islink(x),files)
arg[0] = arg[0] + reduce(lambda x,y:x + y,map(os.path.getsize,files),0)
```

Since the return value of the user-written function is ignored, the total size of the files encountered must be passed through the arg parameter of the

8.7. EXPANSION OF FILENAME WILDCARDS - THE GLOB MODULE125

function. Recall from Section 7.3 that only mutable objects can be modified when passed to a function; thus a list is passed to the function, and the first element of the list is used to accumulate the file sizes. (An alternative would be to use global variables, but the use of such variables should always be avoided when a reasonable alternative exists.) To call the function to sum up the sizes of all the files rooted in the current directory, we would use walk in the following way:

```
total = [0]
dir = '.'
os.path.walk(dir,sumit,total)
print 'Total size of all files rooted at %s: %d bytes' % (dir,total[0])
```

8.7 Expansion of Filename wildcards - the glob module

Under the UNIX operating system, when a filename contains certain symbols, the command shell expands these symbols to represent a list of files that match a specified pattern. For example, if a file name of *.c is passed to the UNIX shell, it will expand the name to represent all of the files in the current directory which end with ".c". In some applications, it would be useful to be able to perform this expansion inside your program, without the need to invoke a shell. The glob module provides the glob function which accepts a filename wildcard expression, and returns a list with the names of all the files which match the expression. One example of glob's use would be to perform filename expansion on the command line for a program designed to run under Windows. A second example would be to find all of the files that begin with a particular string and change that part of the filename to some other string. The wildcard characters which are supported are *, which represents zero or more of any character, ?, which represents exactly one occurence of any character, and a list of characters contained within square brackets ([ ]), which defines a character class similar to the character classes in the re module (Section 8.5). Here's one way to solve the renaming problem, assuming that the old and new strings are passed as the first and second command line arguments, respectively:

```
import sys,glob,re,os
```

126 CHAPTER 8. USING MODULES

```
(old,new) = sys.argv[1:3]
oldre = re.compile(old)
changefiles = glob.glob(old + '*')
for c in changefiles:
os.rename(c,oldre.sub(new,c,count=1))
```

(Reading command line arguments is covered in more detail in Section 8.8.) Keep in mind that under Windows, the glob function is case insensitive,

while under UNIX it is not.

8.8 Information about your Python session - the sys module

Information about the current Python session is provided through a number of variables contained in the sys module. File objects for the three basic input and output streams are stored in the variables stdin (standard input), stdout (standard output), and stderr (standard error); details of their use is presented in Section 5.5.

The array argv contains any arguments which were passed to your python program, if it were called from the command line. The first element of this array (argv[0]) contains the name of the script which is executing, or an empty string if you are entering commands in the python interpreter. (The getopt module can be used to aid in parsing command line flags and arguments.)

The array path contains the names of the directories which will be searched when you use an import statement. If you need to import a module which is stored in a non-standard directory, you can simply append the name of the directory to path before issuing an import command that utilizes the non-standard directory. Keep in mind that the environmental variable PYTHONPATH provides a means for automatically updating the Python system path each time that you invoke Python.

The function object exitfunc will be called immediately before the in-terpreter exits. Note that this is an actual function object, not just the name

8.9. COPYING: THE COPY MODULE

of a function to be called. No arguments should be passed to the function stored in exitfunc.

Finally, the exit function of the sys module allows you to terminate the current Python session. An optional integer argument represents an error code; the value zero is used to indicate normal completion.

8.9 Copying: the copy module

As mentioned in Section 6.1, assignments generally create references to ob-jects, and don't really create a new location in memory containing a copy of the data being assigned. For lists which contain simple data (such as scalar numbers and scalar strings), simply providing a colon in the subscript when copying is sufficient to make a true copy. The copy function of the copy module provides this same capability through a function. Thus, given a list of scalar values, the following two statements are equivalent:

newx = x[:]

newx = copy.copy(x)

If the elements of the object you're trying to copy are not scalars, however, the copy of x stored in newx will actually contain references to the non-scalar objects, and not true copies of those objects. In cases like this, the deepcopy function can be used. This function recursively duplicates all the elements stored in a Python object, and provides a true copy of arbitrary objects in most cases.

As a simple illustration of the difference between copy and deepcopy, consider a list of lists. Note what happens to the two copied objects newx and deepx when an element of one of the nested lists in the original object x is changed:

ft. x = [[1,2,3],['cat','dog','mouse','duck'],[7,8]]

ft. newx = copy.copy(x)

ft. deepx = copy.deepcopy(x)

>>>

ft. x[1][1] = 'gorilla'

ft. newx[1][1]

'gorilla'

ft. deepx[1][1]

'dog'

128 CHAPTER 8. USING MODULES

When we change an element in one of the nested lists of x, that change is reflected in newx, since it simply copied references to each of the nested lists; the value in deepx remains unchanged since it was created with a deep copy. Of course, if we replace an element of the original list, Python will realize that the copies are now the only objects referencing the original value, and both types of copies will retain the original values; the difference between the two methods of copying is only apparent when individual elements of nested objects are modified:

ft. x[2] = [107,108]

ft. newx[2]

[7, 8]

ft. deepx[2] [7, 8]

8.10 Object Persistence: the pickle/cPickle and shelve modules

8.10.1 Pickling

Consider a situation where information is stored in a file, and you've written a Python program to read that file and perform some operation on it. If the contents of the file change regularly, there is usually no recourse but to read the file each time you run your program. But if the contents of the file don't change very often, it may be worthwhile to store the data in a form which is easier for Python to read than plain text. The pickle module takes any Python object and writes it to a file in a format which Python can later read back into memory in an efficient way. On systems that support it, there will also be a cPickle module which is implemented in the C programming language and will generally much faster than the Python implementaion; I'll refer to the cPickle module in the examples that follow. Especially in the case where a large amount of processing needs to be done on a data set to create the Python objects you need, pickling can often make your programs run much faster. In the larger scheme of things, using a database may be a more appropriate solution to achieve persistence. But the pickling approach is very simple, and is adequate for many problems.

There are two steps to the pickling process: first, a Pickler object is

created through a call to the Pickler function. You pass this function a file (or file-like) object, such as that returned by the built-in open function. (See Section 5.4). If you pass Pickler a second argument of 1, it will write the pickled object in a more efficient binary format, instead of the default human-readable format. Having created a Pickler object, you can now invoke the dump method to pickle the object of your choice. At this point, you can invoke the close method on the file object passed to Pickler, or you can let Python close the file when your program terminates.

As a simple example, let's consider a dictionary whose elements are dic-tionaries containing information about employees in a company. Of course, the real benefit of pickling comes when you are creating objects from some large, external data source, but this program will show the basic use of the module:

```
import cPickle,sys
employees = {
'smith':{'firstname':'fred','office':201,'id':'0001','phone':'x232'},
'jones':{'firstname':'sue','office':207,'id':'0003','phone':'x225'},
'williams':{'firstname':'bill','office':215,'id':'0004','phone':'x219'}}
try:
f = open('employees.dump','w')
except IOError:
print >>sys.stderr, 'Error opening employees.dump for write' sys.exit(1)
pkl = cPickle.Pickler(f,1)
pkl.dump(employees)
```

When the employee dictionary is needed in another program, all we need to do is open the file containing the pickled object, and use the load function of the cPickle module:

ft. import cPickle

ft. f = open('employees.dump','r')

ft. employees = cPickle.load(f)

ft. employees['jones']['office']

207

ft. employees['smith']['firstname']

'fred'

Pickling can offer an especially attractive alternative to databases when you've created a class which represents a complex data structure. (Sec-tion 10.4).

8.10.2 The shelve module

Notice that to create a pickled object the entire object must be in memory; similarly, when you unpickle an object, you must read the entire object into memory. When you're dealing with very large amounts of data, the shelve module may provide a better alternative. (It should be noted that interfacing to a relational database may be a more useful solution in some cases. There are a number of Python modules available to access many different databases; see http://www.python.org/topics/database/modules.html for more in-formation.) The shelve module creates a persistent, file-based version of an object very similar to a Python dictionary, but data is only read from or written to the file when necessary, for example when you need to access a value stored in the file, or add a value to the file. One limitation of shelve objects is that the keys to the objects must be strings, but the values stored in a shelve object can be any Python object, as long as it can be written with the pickle module.

To create a shelve object, use the open function from the shelve module, providing the name of a file to be used to hold the shelve object. The shelve module may call another program which will create more than one file, but the open method will always find your shelved object when you refer to the filename that was used when you first open the shelve object. If the file you specify already exists, but is not a shelve object created in a previous program, you'll get a anydbm.error exception; otherwise the open function will recognize a previously shelved object and open it. Since information is written to the shelved object only when necessary, it's important to invoke the close method on any shelved objects you use to insure that changes that you make during your program are properly stored.

Here's the employee example revisited, using a shelve object. While there's not much advantage in shelving over pickling for such a small data set, it will illustrate the basic ideas of using a shelve object.

```
>>> import shelve
```



```
>>> employees = {
... 'smith':{'firstname':'fred','office':201,'id':'0001','phone':'x232'},
... 'jones':{'firstname':'sue','office':207,'id':'0003','phone':'x225'},
... 'williams':{'firstname':'bill','office':215,'id':'0004',
... 'phone':'x219'}}
>>> try:
... emp = shelve.open('employees.dat')
... except IOError:
... print >> sys.stderr, 'Error opening employees.dat'
... sys.exit(1)
...
>>> for k in employees:
... emp[k] = employees[k]
...
>>> emp.close()
```

When we need to access the shelved data, we simply open the appropriate file, and the data will be available:

```
>>> import shelve
>>> employees = shelve.open('employees.dat')
>>> employees['jones']['office']
207
```

ft. employees['smith']['firstname']

'fred'

ft.

8.11 CGI (Common Gateway Interface): the cgi module

8.11.1 Introduction to CGI

When you type the address of a web page (i.e. a URL or Universal Resource Locator) into a browser,or click a link which refers to a URL, a request is made to a computer on the internet to send the contents of a web page to your browser. Web pages are written in a language known as HTML (Hy-pertext Markup Language), and your web browser knows how to translate HTML into text, pictures, links, animations or whatever else the designer

132 CHAPTER 8. USING MODULES

of the web page had in mind. Alternatively, the address that your browser requests might be a program, in which case that program will be run on the web site's computer, and the results of the program (most likely a header followed by something written in HTML) will be transmitted to your web browser. Through the use of forms or specially formatted URLs, you can pro-vide information to that program, allowing on-line shopping, surveys, email programs and other useful tools. CGI is the name given to the mechanism used to transmit information to and from your web browser and a web site's computer. The cgi module provides a way for you to retrieve this informa-tion, and to send HTML back in response to a submitted form.

Besides using a form which displays in a browser to retrieve information, a specialized type of URL can be used to transmit information to a web site's computer. When this method is used, the program's name is followed by a question mark and a series of name=value pairs separated by ampersands. For example, a URL to query a travel agency might look like this:

http://www.travelagency.com/cgi-bin/query?dest=Costa%20Rica&month=Jun&day=12

In this case, three variables are being transmitted: dest with a value of "Costa Rica"; month, with a value of "Jun" and day, with a value of "12". (Notice that special characters like blanks need to be encoded as a percent sign followed by two digits.) Alternatively, there might be a form with drop-down menus, scrolling lists, or blanks to be filled in which would extract the same information.

When you use a Python script as a CGI program, you create a FieldStorage object using the FieldStorage function of the cgi module. This object be-haves like a dictionary in many ways. For example, you can use the keys method to get a list of all the variables which were sent to your program. When you use any of these names as an index to the object returned by FieldStorage, the result is a MiniFieldStorage object, which contains two attributes: name and value. Thus, if the following Python program were properly installed on the fictitious travel bureau's web server, it would print the destination, month and day specified in the URL:

```
import cgi
f = cgi.FieldStorage()
print "Content-type: text/html"
```

8.11. CGI (COMMON GATEWAY INTERFACE): THE CGI MODULE133

```
print
vars = f.keys()
for v in vars:
print '%s = %s<br>' % (v,f[v].value)
```

The two print statements before the loop produce the header which is nec-essary for a browser to understand that what follows will be HTML which needs to be appropriately processed before being displayed; the second of these print statements produces a blank line which signals that the headers are finished. The value of each of the variables transmitted through the CGI program is stored in the value attribute of the MiniFieldStorage object stored in the FieldStorage object named f. Since newlines are not respected by HTML, the <br> tag is used to insure that a line break appears between the values displayed.

Alternatively, information can be transmitted to a CGI program through from items which appear in your browser. The URL of the CGI program appears in the action element of the <form> tag. The following (minimal) HTML code will display the form shown in Figure 8.1; when the user makes their selection and presses the “Submit” button, the CGI script presented above will receive the information; the FieldStorage object will be created appropriately whether the input comes from a URL or through a form.

```
<html>
<body>
<form method="post" action="/cgi-bin/query">
Destination: <input type="text" name="dest" size=40>
Month: <select name=month>
<option>Jan<option>Feb<option>Mar<option>Apr<option>May
<option>Jun<option>Jul<option>Aug<option>Sep<option>Oct
<option>Nov<option>Dec</select>
Day: <select name=day>
<option>1<option>2<option>3<option>4<option>5<option>6<option>7
<option>8<option>9<option>10<option>11<option>12 <option>13
<option>14<option>15<option>16<option>17<option>18<option>19
<option>20<option>21<option>22<option>23<option>24<option>25
<option>26<option>27<option>28<option>29<option>30<option>31
</select>
```

134 CHAPTER 8. USING MODULES

Figure 8.1: Simple HTML form

```
<center>
<input type=submit>
</center>
</form>
</body>
</html>
```

8.11.2 Security Concerns

If you write a CGI script that accepts information from the outside world, and then uses that information to access another program (through, for example the system function of the os module), it’s very important to make sure that you don’t inadvertently send a malicious command to the operating system. There are two things that will minimize the risk of this happening. First, make sure that your CGI program has access to only the minimum set of programs it needs by using a very simple command path; on unix, a line like the following in your CGI script will serve this purpose.

```
os.environ['PATH'] = '/bin:/usr/bin'
```

Secondly, you should insure that any variables which are transmitted to your program and will be used as part of an operating system command do not contain any special characters; that is, they are composed of letters, digits and the underscore only. Regular expressions (Section 8.5) can be used to test this. For example, the following function ensures that any word passed to it contains no special characters:

```
def chkname(name,extra=''):
valid = r'\w'
if extra:
valid = r'[' + valid + extra + r']'
```

Name
Contents
HTTP
COOKIE
Persistent data stored in cookies
HTTP
REFERER
URL of refering document
HTTP
USER
AGENT
Type of browser being used
QUERY
STRING
URL Fragment after ?
REMOTE
ADDR
IP Address of user
REMOTE
HOST
Hostname of user
REMOTE
USER
Username, if authentication was used
SERVER
NAME
Hostname of server
SERVER
PORT
Port number of server
SERVER
SOFTWARE
Name and version of server software
Table 8.6: Some Environmental Variables Passed through CGI

```
if re.match(r'^%s+$' % valid,name):
return 1
else return 2
```

To accommodate common email addresses, extra='@.' could be passed to chkname

8.11.3 CGI Environmental Variables

In addition to information which is transmitted through CGI variables (like dest, month and day in the previous example), a large amount of information is transfered to CGI programs through environmental variables. These variables can be accessed in your program in the usual way, that is, by using the eviron dictionary of the os module. Table 8.6 lists the names and meanings of some of these environmental variables.

8.12 Accessing Documents on the Web: the
urllib module

While the cgi module is useful on the server side of the World Wide Web, the urlopen is useful when developing applications that act as clients to the World Wide Web. While Python can be written to write full scale browsers (see the Grail project at http://grail.sourceforge.net), the

136 CHAPTER 8. USING MODULES

urllib module is most useful when writing applications that try to auto-mate interaction with the web.

The core of the module is the urlopen function. This function accepts a URL as an argument, and returns a file-like object which allows you to access the contents of the URL using any of the standard file methods (read, readline, or readlines; see Section 5.4.1 for details). An optional second argument is a url-encoded string (see the urlencode function below) which provides data to be sent to the URL if it is a CGI program. If the URL provided does not begin with a http:// or ftp://, the request is treated as a local file.

As a simple example of the use of the urlopen function, the CNN web site, http://www.cnn.com, displays the top headline in a prominent font; at the time of this writing, the top headline can be indentified as the anchor on a line identified with a class of cnnMainT1Headline. Since the headline is an active link, it is surrounded by anchor tags, i.e. <a> or <A> and </a> or </A>. We can write a regular expression to extract the headline from these tags:

```
headlinepat = re.compile(r'<.*cnnMainT1Headline.*><a.*>(.*)</a>',re.I)
```

All that remains is to access the contents of the page with the urllopen function:

```
try:
f = urllib.urlopen('http://www.cnn.com')
except IOError:
sys.stderr.write("Couldn't connect to CNN website\n")
sys.exit(1)
contents = f.read()
headline = headlinepat.findall(contents)
print headline[0]
```

Since findall returns a list, only the first element of the list is printed.

The urlopen function can also be used to post data to a CGI program. The information to be posted can either be embedded in the URL itself, or it can be sent to the URL through headers. In the first case, it is important to make sure that special characters (blanks, punctuation, etc.) are converted to the appropriate codes using the quote function of the urllib module. In

8.12. ACCESSING DOCUMENTS ON THE WEB: THE URLLIB MODULE137

the second case, the urlencode function accepts a dictionary of values, and converts them to the appropriate form:

```
ft. travelplans = {'dest': 'Costa Rica','month': 'Jun','day' : 25}

ft. urllib.urlencode(travelplans)

'month=Jun&day=25&dest=Costa+Rica'
```

We could contact the fictitious travel agency CGI program in Section 8.11.1 with a program like this one:

```
urllib.urlopen('http://www.travelagency.com/cgi-bin/query',\ urllib.urlencode(travelplans))
```

As a more realistic example, many websites offer stock quotes, by accept-ing a company's ticker tape symbol as part of a query string specified in their URL. One such example is http://www.quote.com; to display a page of information about a stock with ticker tape symbol xxx, you could point your browser to

http://finance.lycos.com/home/stocks/quotes.asp?symbols=xxx

Examination of the HTML text returned by this URL shows that the current quote is the first bold (i.e. between <b> and </b> tags) text on the line following a line with the time at which the quote was issued. We can extract a current quote for a stock with the following function:

```
import sys,re,urllib
def getquote(symbol):
lspat = re.compile('\d?\d:\d\d[ap]m .+T')
boldpat = re.compile('<b>(.*?)</b>',re.I)
```

url = 'http://finance.lycos.com/home/stocks/quotes.asp?symbols=%s' % \ symbol
f = urllib.urlopen(url)
lastseen = 0
while 1:
line = f.readline()
if not line : break
if lastseen:
quote = boldpat.findall(line)[0]
138 CHAPTER 8. USING MODULES
break
if lspat.search(line):
lastseen = 1
return quote

The syntax of the URLs accepted by urlopen allows embedding a user-name/password pair or optional port number in the URL. Suppose we wish to access the site http://somesite.com, using user name myname and pass-word secret, through port 8080 instead of the usual default of 80. The following call to urlopen could be used:

urllib.urlopen('http://myname:secret@somesite.com:8080')

A similar scheme can be used to access files on FTP (File Transfer Protocol) servers. For more control over FTP, Python also provides the ftplib module.

Chapter 9 Exceptions

9.1 Introduction

One of the basic principles of Python mentioned in Chapter 1 was the idea of exception handling. Unlike many languages, which leave the business of error handling to the programmer using the language, Python handles errors in a consistent way – when an error is encountered, Python prints a descriptive message, and terminates execution. But beyond this default behaviour, Python provides a simple way to trap these errors and either ignore them, fix them, or decide that program termination really is the best idea. The basic notion of the try/except clause has already been introduced; in this chapter we'll discuss its use more thoroughly, as well as look at how to create new exceptions, and how to raise exceptions within your programs.

9.2 Tracebacks

Whenever you use a try/except clause, the programming statements con-tained in the try portion of the code are executed in a "protected" environ-ment, in the sense that errors occurring in that code will not cause python to terminate. Instead, you have the opportunity to catch and examine the error, and take the action of your choice. Perhaps the most classic example of the try/except clause is to catch problems when you attempt to open a file. Let's take a look at what happens when we try to open a file that doesn't exist:

>>> f = open('not.a.file')
139
140 CHAPTER 9. EXCEPTIONS
Traceback (innermost last):
File "<stdin>", line 1, in ?
IOError: [Errno 2] No such file or directory: 'not.a.file'

The traceback provided by Python contains useful information. First, the line and file in which the error was encountered is displayed. While this is not of much use in an interactive session, it is invaluable when running your Python programs from a file. The final line of the traceback is especially important when considering how to deal with problems that might arise in your program, since it gives the name of the exception which was encountered. Many exceptions also provide specific information about the nature of the exception, like the "No such file or directory" message in this example. You can capture this additional information in a variable by specifying the name of that variable after the name of the exception you're catching, separated by a comma.

>>> try:

```
... f = open('not.a.file')
... except IOError,msg:
... print msg
...
[Errno 2] No such file or directory: 'not.a.file'
```

If Python encountered this code in a program it was executing, the program would not terminate after failing to open the file, since the IOError was trapped. In many situations, you'll want to terminate your program when you encounter an exception, by calling the exit function of the sys module (See Section 8.8 for details.)

9.3 Dealing with Multiple Exceptions

Although it is often common to have just a few statements as part of a try/except clause, you may want to run a larger section of code in such a clause, and then organize all the exception handling after that block of code. As a simple example, suppose we have a dictionary, mapping user's names to the location of a file with information about the user. Given a user's name, our program will look up the file name in the dictionary, and then print the file. In the course of doing this, two different exceptions may arise. First, if

9.3. DEALING WITH MULTIPLE EXCEPTIONS

141

the user is not in the dictionary, then a KeyError exception will be raised; if the file can't be open, then an IOError exception will be raised. First, here's a code fragment that catches both of these errors in a single except clause:

```
userdict = {'john':'/home/john/infofile', 'sue':'/users/sue/sue.info', 'fred':'/home/fred/info.fred'}
user = 'joe'
try:
thefile = userdict[user]
print open(thefile).read()
except (KeyError,IOError):
sys.stderr.write('Error getting information for %s\n' % user)
```

Alternatively, each exception can be dealt with individually.

```
try:
thefile = userdict[user]
print open(thefile).read()
except KeyError:
sys.stderr.write('No information for %s is available\n' % user)
except IOError,msg:
sys.stderr.write('Error opening %s: %s\n' % (thefile,msg)
```

When you use multiple except clauses, Python will execute the code in the first clause it encounters for which that exception is true, and then execute the code after the entire try/except construction. Notice that any exception other than a KeyError or IOError will be handled in the usual way, namely Python will print a traceback and exit. You can catch all types of errors by including an except statement with no exception name, but this practice should generally be avoided, since all exceptions, including syntax errors, incorrect function calls and misspelled variable names, will be trapped by such a statement. In general, different errors need different remedies, and part of proper exception handling consists of determining exactly what should be done when different errors are encountered.

142 CHAPTER 9. EXCEPTIONS

9.4 The Exception Hierarchy

When you have several except clauses as part of a try/except construct, and an exception is raised, the statements after the first except clause which is matched will be executed. Usually this will not cause any surprises, but there is a hierarchy of exceptions in Python so that exceptions higher in the hierarchy will be activated even though they are not an exact match for the exception that has been raised. For example, the EnvironmentError exception will catch both IOErrors and OSErrors. Thus, when you cre-ate try/except clauses in your programs, the ordering of the exceptions may affect they way that their corresponding code is called. Continuing with the EnvironmentError example, if an except clause for an OSError appeared after an except clause for an EnvironmentError within the same try/except construction, the OSError clause would never be activated, since the EnvironmentError would intercept the exception, and only one excep-tion per try/except construct will ever be activated. On the other hand, if the EnvironmentError clause appeared after the OSError clause, it would be activated when an IOError was raised, since that exception is below EnvironmentError in the exception hierarchy. Figure 9.1 illustrates the hi-erarchy; exceptions which are indented below other exceptions will be caught by the less indented exception as well as through their own names.

9.5 Raising Exceptions

In addition to responding to exceptions in other programs, you can raise exceptions in your own programs.

You can raise any of the existing exceptions, or you can create new ones of your own. Figure 9.1 lists all the built-in exceptions; you can also find their names by examining the directory of the __builtins__ object; all the exceptions contain the string "Error" or "Exit".

You can create your own exceptions as subclasses of the built in Exception class. (Creating and working with classes is described in detail in Chap-ter 10.4.) To create a new exception called MyError, the following code can be used:

class MyError(Exception):

pass

9.5. RAISING EXCEPTIONS 143

Exception
StandardError
Arithmetic Error
FloatingPointError
OverflowError
ZeroDivisionError
AssertionError
AttributeError
EnvironmentError
IOError
OSError
EOFError
ImportError
KeyBoardInterrupt
LookupError
IndexError
KeyError
MemoryError
NameError
RuntimeError
SyntaxError
SystemExit
TypeError
ValueError

Figure 9.1: Exception Hierarchy

144 CHAPTER 9. EXCEPTIONS

The pass statement serves as a placeholder in situations when Python ex-pects a statement, but you don't need to do anything. No further details are needed to create a usable exception.

After creating an exception, you can use the raise statement to activate it. Suppose we are writing a function which will create an archive of files on a 100Mb zip disk. Before writing the archive, we will check to make sure that all the files will fit on the disk; if they will not, we'll raise a SizeError exception. In this way, the calling program can decide on what action is appropriate. Here is the code to define the exception and create the archive:

```
import shutil,os
class SizeError(Exception):
pass
def mkarchive(dir,capacity=100*1024*1024):
files = os.listdir(dir)
totalsize = 0
for f in files:
totalsize = totalsize + os.getsize(os.path.join(dir,f))
if totalsize > capacity:
raise SizeError(dir)
for f in files:
shutil.copy(os.path.join(dir,f),os.path.join('/zip',f))
```

Note that the copy function may very well raise exceptions of its own; how-ever, since we've defined our own SizeError exception, we'll be able to distinguish between the two types of error.

Now consider how we might use this function. Suppose that we're going to create several archives, with a program that will prompt us to change disks between each archive. The following program would repeatedly call the mkarchive function, printing appropriate status messages after each call:

```
dirs = ['/home/joe/papers','/home/sue/backup','/home/fred/save'] for d in dirs:
print 'Insert zip disk and hit return ', sys.stdin.readline()
```

9.5. RAISING EXCEPTIONS

145

```
try:
mkarchive(dir)
print 'Archived %s to zip disk' % dir except SizeError,msg:
print 'Directory %s too large for zip disk' % msg except IOError,msg:
print 'Error archiving directory %s : %s' % (dir,msg)
```

Notice that the print statement after the call to mkarchive will only be executed if no exception was encountered in the function call.

While it's natural to think of raising exceptions when an error is detected, exceptions can be used in other situations as well. Recall the walk function introduced in Section 8.6. This function will traverse a directory, calling a user-written function each time a new directory is encountered. Suppose we wish to write a program to search for a file with a particular name, but we'd like the program to stop searching as soon as it finds such a file. While we could exit the program entirely (by calling sys.exit), there's no way to simply return from the walk function until all the directories have been traversed without exceptions. We could create an exception, raise that exception once the filename has been found, and put the call to walk inside a try/except loop. The following program implements that strategy.

```
import os
class FoundException(Exception):
pass
def chkname(name,dir,files):
if name in files:
raise FoundException(os.path.join(dir,name))
name = 'errno.h'
startdir = '/usr/include'
try:
os.path.walk(startdir,chkname,name)
```

```
print '%s not found starting at %s' % (name,startdir)
except FoundException,pathname:
print '%s found: %s' % (name,pathname)
```

146 CHAPTER 9. EXCEPTIONS

A similar strategy can be employed to make a "panic" exit from inside of deeply-nested loops.

Chapter 10

Writing Modules

10.1 Introduction

In Python, a module is simply a file which contains Python code and which can be imported into some other program. Thus, if you have a collection of functions which you'd like to use in other python programs, you can simply put them all in one file, say myfunctions.py, and use the import statement to make those functions available to you. If your module is located in your working directory, Python will always find it. Otherwise, it must be located in Python's search path. You can view the search path with the following Python statements:

```
import sys
sys.path
```

Since sys.path is just a list, you can append the names of other directories to search onto this list before using an import statement, to allow you to access modules which are not on the search path. But if you keep your mod-ules in one location, a more useful approach may be to set the PYTHONPATH environmental variable to that location in the appropriate startup file for your operating system. That way, all the Python programs you run will be able to use your modules.

147

148 **CHAPTER 10. WRITING MODULES**

10.2 An Example

As a simple example of a module, we'll write three functions which would be useful if you were working with files. The first, which we'll call lline, will return the length of the longest line encountered in a file. The second, which we'll call wcount will be a python version of the UNIX command wc, which, given a file name, returns the number of lines, words and characters contained in the file. The final function, which we'll call ccount, will count the number of occurences of a given character in a file. To make these functions available for use in programs, we'll store the python code for these three functions in a file called fileutil.py, stored in either the current directory, or one of the directories in the python search path. The following code implements these three functions:

```
def lline(filename):
f = open(filename,'r')
longest = 0
for line in f:
lennow = len(line) - 1
if lennow > longest:
longest = lennow
f.close()
return longest
def wcount(filename):
f = open(filename,'r')
nlines = nwords = nchars = 0
for line in f:
nlines = nlines + 1
nwords = nwords + len(line.split())
nchars = nchars + len(line)
f.close()
return (nlines,nwords,nchars)
```

```
def ccount(filename,char='\t'):
f = open(filename,'r')
found = 0
for line in f:
```



```
found = found + line.count(char)
f.close()
return found
```

A few comments on the design of these functions is in order. Notice that, unlike previous examples, the calls to open are not enclosed in a try/except clause. Since these functions are designed to be imported into a program which will call them, the decision was made to allow any exceptions which are raised to "filter up" to the calling program, where the programmer who was calling the functions would be expected to deal with them This is a decision which should not be ignored when designing a module; in the current example, since there's not much that these functions can do if they can't open the file that was passed to them, the decision to pass the responsibility of dealing with exceptions to the caller of the function seemed reasonable. In other cases, it might be more appropriate to trap the exception, especially when some useful alternative in the face of the exception is possible.

In the lline function, the newline was not included in the length of the longest line – in practice, it might be more useful to pass another argument to the function which would allow you to include the newline in the reported length.

In the ccount function, the default character to search for is defined to be a tab. This is an arbitrary choice, but it would make the function easy to use when trying to decide whether or not to use white space or tabs as a separator when reading data from a file. For other situations, a different default character might be more reasonable.

To use these functions, we can simply import them in the usual way (provided they reside in a directory on python's search path.) For example, to check a list of files passed on the command line to insure that none of them have any lines longer than 80 characters, we could write a program like the following one:

```
#!/usr/local/bin/python
import sys,fileutil
for file in sys.argv[1:]:

cv.  = fileutil.lline(file) if ll > 80:

print 'Long line (%d chars) found in %s' % (ll,file)
```


If you only needed one function from the module, individual functions could be imported from fileutil in the usual way (See Section 8.2). In fact, once you've written a module in Python, and that module's directory is on the Python search path, there's very little difference between a user-written module and a module that's a part of Python itself.

10.3 Test Programs for Modules

When you write a collection of functions, it's a very good idea to write a test program, to make sure that the functions are doing what you expect. That way, if you decide to make changes to the functions at some point in the future, you can quickly check to see if the functions still work. Of course, one way to create a test program would be to write the program in a separate file from the module itself. However, Python provides a convenient way to keep your test program in the same file as the module itself.

Remember that when you import a module into a Python program that the contents of the module are executed when the import statement is en-countered. Thus, you can't just include your test program in your module, or it will be executed every time the module is imported. But Python pro-vides a builtin variable called __name__, which will be equal to the name of a module when the module is imported, but will be equal to the value "__main__" when a program is executed directly. Thus, we could include a test program for the strfunc module by including the following lines in the file strfunc.py after the function definitions:

if __name__ == '__main__':

import sys

files = sys.argv[1:]

for f in files:

print 'Processing %s' % f

print ' Longest line is %d characters' % lline(f)

print ' File contains %d lines, %d words, and %d characters' % wcount(print ' The file contains %d spaces' % ccount(f,' ') print

Now when the program is invoked directly (for example through the execfile function, or by typing the program's name at a shell prompt), the test pro-

10.4. CLASSES AND OBJECT ORIENTED PROGRAMMING

151

gram will be run, but when the module is imported into another program, the test program is ignored. Notice that in this example, since the sys module is not needed for the functions defined in the fileutil module, the import statement for that module was placed after the if statement which checks for the value of __name__.

10.4 Classes and Object Oriented Program-ming

Creating a module with a set of functions to perform useful tasks is certainly an effective way to approach many problems. If you find that this approach can solve all your problems, you may be content to use it and not explore other possible ways of getting things done. However, Python provides a simple method for implementing object oriented programming through the use of classes. We've already seen situations where we've taken advantage of these ideas through the methods available for manipulating lists, dictionaries and file objects. File objects in particular show the power of these techniques. Once you create a file object, it doesn't matter where it came from - when you want to, say, read a line from such an object, you simply invoke the readline method. The ability to do what you want without having to worry about the internal details is a hallmark of object oriented programming. The main tool in Python for creating objects is the class statement. When you create a class, it can contain variables (often called attributes in this context) and methods. To actually create an object that you can use in your programs, you invoke the name of its class; in object oriented lingo we say that the class name serves as a constructor for the object. Methods are defined in a similar way to functions with one small difference. When you define a method, the first argument to the method should be called self, and it represents the object upon which the method is acting. Even though self is in the argument list, you don't explicitly pass an object name through this argument. Instead, as we've seen for builtin methods, you follow the name of the object with a period and the method name and argument list.

152

CHAPTER 10. WRITING MODULES

Method

Use

__init__(object)

called when class constructor is invoked

__repr__(object)

also called when object name typed in interpre

__del__(object)

called when an object is destroyed

__str__(object)

called by print(object)

__len__(object)

called by len(object)

__getitem__(object,key)

allows you to intercept subscripting requests

__setitem__(object,key,value)
allows you to set values of subscripted items
__getslice__(object,start,fin)
allows you to intercept slice requests
__setslice__(object,start,fin,value)
allows you to set slices
__add__(object,other)
called by object + other
__radd__(object,other)
called by other + object
__sub__(object,other)
called by object - other
__mul__(object,other)
called by object * other
__mod__(object,other)
called by object % other
Table 10.1: Methods for Operator Overloading

10.5 Operator Overloading

Besides creating methods of our own, we can change the meaning of the way that many familiar operators work, a technique known as operator overload-ing. Special methods, whose names begin and end with double underscores, can be defined to "intercept" many common operators, allowing you to rede-fine what such operators as print, + and * or functions like len will do when they're applied to the objects you create. One of the most important oper-ator overloading methods is the __init__ method. This method is called whenever the class name is used as a constructor, and allows you to initialize attributes in your object at the same time as you create it. The __str__ method is called through the print statement; the __repr__ method is called when an object's name is typed in the interpreter. Table 10.1 lists some of the more commonly used methods for overloading.

In addition, you can define what happens when your object is iterated over by means of the for statement by defining an __iter__ method that simply returns the object itself, and providing a next method which will be called for each iteration. Inside the next method, you need to raise a StopIteration exception when no more items are available. (See Section 10.10 for an exam-ple.

10.6. PRIVATE ATTRIBUTES

153

10.6 Private Attributes

In many object-oriented languages, certain attributes can be declared as private, making it impossible for users of a class to directly view or modify their values. The designer of the class then provides methods to control the ways in which these attributes can be manipulated. While Python classes don't have true private attributes, if an attribute name begins with two underscores, the Python interpreter internally modifies the attribute's name, so that references to the attribute will not be resolved. (Of course anyone willing to look up the way in which the attribute name is "mangled" could still access it.) Through this convention, you can create attributes which will only be available within the methods you define for the class, giving you more control over the way users of your class will manipulate those attributes.

10.7 A First Example of Classes

To clarify these ideas, we'll consider a simple example – an "interactive" database of phone numbers and email addresses. To get started with de-signing a class, it's often easiest to think about the information you're going to manipulate when you eventually operate on that class. You don't need to think of everything the first time you create the class; one of the many attractive features of working with classes is that you can easily modify them as you get deeper into solving a problem. In the case of our database, the basic information we'll be storing will be a name, an phone number and an email address. We'll call the class that will hold this information Friend, and when we actually store our information it will be in what is generically known as an object; in this case a Friend object. We can define methods by indenting their definitions under the class statement.

When we create a Friend object, all we need to do is store the name, phone number and email address of a friend, so the __init__ method will be very simple – we just need to create three attributes which we'll call name, phone and email. This object will serve as a building block for our database, so we don't need to define many other methods. As an example, we'll create a __str__ method, and an identical __repr__ method so that we can display information about our friends in a readable format.

```
>>> class Friend:
... def __init__(self,name,phone='',email=''):
154
CHAPTER 10.
WRITING MODULES
...
...
...
...
...
self.name = name
self.phone = phone
self.email = email
def __str__(self):
return 'Name: %s\nPhone: %s\nEmail: %s' % \
(self.name,self.phone,self.email)
... def __repr__(self):
... return self.__str__()
...
```

ft. x = Friend('Joe Smith','555-1234','joe.smith@notmail.com')

ft. y = Friend('Harry Jones','515-2995','harry@who.net')

ft. print x

```
Name: Joe Smith
Phone: 555-1234
Email: joe.smith@notmail.com
>>> y
Name: Harry Jones
Phone: 515-2995
Email: harry@who.net
```

Just as with functions, we can provide default values for arguments passed to methods. In this case, name is the only required argument; the other two arguments default to empty strings. Notice that attributes are refered to as self.name; without the leading self, variables will be treated as local, and will not be stored with the object. Finally, notice that the print operator as well as the interactive session's default display have been overridden with the __str__ and __repr__ methods, respectively.

Now, we can create a database containing information about our friends, through the Frienddb class. To make it useful, we'll introduce persistence through the cPickle module introduced in Section 8.10.1. When we first create the database, we'll require the name of a file. If the file exists, we'll assume it's a database we've already created and work with that; if the file doesn't exist, we'll open it and prepare it to receive our pickled database. For this simple application, we can simply create a list of Friend objects, and store the list as an attribute in our Frienddb object.

When designing an object oriented application like this, we simply need to identify the operations we'll want to do on the object we've created. In addition to the __init__ method, some of the tasks we'd want to implement

would be adding a new friend to the database, searching the database for information about a particular person, and storing the database when we're done with it. (In the following sections, it's assumed that the class definition for Friend is either in the same file as the Frienddb definition or has been properly imported along with the other appropriate modules (os,cPickle, sys,re and string). In addition, the following class statement will have appeared before the definition of these methods:

```
class Frienddb:
```

The __init__ method for our database will take care of all the dealings with the file in which the database will be stored.

```
import sys
class Frienddb:
def __init__(self,file=None):
if file == None:
print 'Must provide a filename'
return
self.file = file
if os.path.isfile(file):
try:
f = open(file,'r')
except IOError:
sys.stderr.write('Problem opening file %s\n' % file)
return
try:
self.db = cPickle.load(f)
return
except cPickle.UnpicklingError:
print >>sys.stderr, '%s is not a pickled database.' % file return
f.close()
else:
self.db = []
```

Since the __init__ statement acts as a constructor for class objects, it should never return a value. Thus, when errors are encountered, a return statement with no value must be used. This method puts two attributes into our

Frienddb object: file, the name of the file to store the database, and db, the list containing Friend objects (if the database already exists) or an empty list if there is not a file with the name passed to the method.

The method for adding an entry to the database is simple:

```
def add(self,name,phone='',email=''):
self.db.append(Friend(name,phone,email))
```

Searching the database is a little more complex. We'll use the re mod-ule (Section 8.5) to allow regular expression searches, and return a list of Friend objects whose name attributes match the pattern which is provided. Since we'll be searching each name in the database, the regular expression is compiled before being used.

```
def search(self,pattern):
srch = re.compile(pattern,re.I)
```

```
found = []
for item in self.db:
if srch.search(item.name):
found.append(item)
return found
```

Finally, we'll write methods to store the contents of the database into the file that was specified when the database was created. This is just a straightfor-ward use of the cPickle module (Section 8.10.1). To insure that data is not lost, a __del__ method which simply calls the store method (provided that there were entries in the database) will be added as well:

```
def store(self):
try:
f = open(self.file,'w')
except IOError:
print >>sys.stderr, \
'Problem opening file %s for write\n' % self.file
return
p = cPickle.Pickler(f,1)
p.dump(self.db)
f.close()
def __del__(self):
```



```
if self.db:
self.store()
```

Having created these two classes, we can now write a simple program to use them. You might want to include such a program in the file containing the class definitions; if so, see Section 10.3. We'll write a small interactive program that will recognize three commands: "a", which will cause the program to prompt for a name, phone number and email address and the add it to the database, "? pattern", which will print all the records whose name attribute matches pattern, and q, which will store the database and exit. In the program that follows, I'm assuming that the class definitions for Friend and Frienddb are stored in a file called frienddb.py which is in a directory on the python search path.

```
import frienddb
file = raw_input('File? ')
fdb = Frienddb(file)
while 1:
line = raw_input('> ')
if line[0] == 'a':
name = raw_input('Name? ')
phone = raw_input('Phone number? ')
email = raw_input('Email? ')
fdb.add(name,phone,email)
elif line[0] == '?':
line = string.strip(line[1:])
fdb.search(line)
elif line[0] == 'q':
fdb.store()
break
```

Other methods could be implemented as well. While not necessarily that useful, suppose we wanted to access elements of our database either by a numeric index, indicating their position in the database, or by the name attribute of the individual records. Using the __getitem__ method, we could subscript the database just as we do lists or dictionaries. To properly process both string and numeric indices, we'd need to distinguish between these two types of values. One way to do this is by trying an numeric conversion of the

158 CHAPTER 10. WRITING MODULES

index with the int function; if an exception is thrown, then we must have a string value.

```
def __getitem__(self,key):
try:
index = int(key)
return self.db[index]
except ValueError:
found = 0
for item in self.db:
if item.name == key:
return item
raise KeyError(key)
```

If a string is given, and no record with that name is found, the method simply raises the builtin KeyError exception, allowing the caller of the method to decide how to handle this case. Now we can access the database through subscripts:

ft. import frienddb

ft. fdb = frienddb.Frienddb('friend.db')

ft. fdb[0]

Name: Harry Smith
Phone: 443-2199
Email: hsmith@notmail.com

ft. fdb[1] Name: Sue Jones Phone: 332-1991 Email: sue@sue.net

ft. fdb['Harry Smith'] Name: Harry Smith Phone: 443-2199

Email: hsmith@notmail.com

10.8 Inheritance

One of the biggest benefits of the class-based approach to programming is that classes can inherit attributes and methods from other classes. If you

10.8. INHERITANCE

159

need to work with an object that's very similar to some other object that has already been developed, your new object can inherit all of the old object's methods, add new ones, and/or overwrite the ones which need to change.

Continuing with our little database example, suppose that you found the friend database so useful at home, that you'd like to extend it into a database to keep track of business contacts. It would be very helpful to have a few additional fields in the database, let's say a company name and the type of product that the company produces. Following the example of the Friend object, we could create a Contact object as follows:

class Contact:

```
def __init__(self,name,company,phone='',email='',product=''):
self.name = name
self.company = company
self.phone = phone
self.email = email
self.product = product
def __str__(self):
return 'Name: %s\nCompany: %s\nPhone: %s\nEmail: %s\nProduct: %s' % \
(self.name,self.company,self.phone,self.email,self.product)
def __repr__(self):
return self.__str__()
```

Now we'd like to create an object that would let us store, add and search a database of contacts. The details of opening files, pickling, searching, and indexing really haven't changed – our Contactdb object can simply inherit all of them from the Frienddb object. The only real change is that now we'll be storing Contact objects in the list called db inside of the object instead of Friend objects, so we'll need to overwrite the add method:

```
from frienddb import Frienddb
class Contactdb(Frienddb):
def add(self,name,company,phone='',email='',product=''):
self.db.append(Contact(name,company,phone,email,product))
```

160 CHAPTER 10. WRITING MODULES

By putting the name of another class (Frienddb) in parentheses after the name of our new class (Contactdb) we're informing Python that this class will inherit methods and attributes from that old class. If we invoke a method or try to access an attribute that's been explicitly defined for our new class, Python will use the one we've defined. But if we refer to a method or attribute we haven't explicitly defined, it will refer to that method or attribute in the so-called "parent" class. (Python even supports multiple inheritance; if you have a comma-separated list of classes in parentheses after your class name, python will search each of them in turn for methods or attributes not explicitly defined for the new class.) Thus after simply defining the add method, we can create and use our contact database:

ft. import contactdb

ft. fdb.search('harry') [Name: Harry Smith Phone: 443-2199

Email: hsmith@notmail.com]

ft. cdb = contactdb.Contactdb('new.db')

ft. cdb.add('Mary Wilson','Brainpower, Inc.','222-3292',

...'mw@brainpower.net','consulting')

ft. cdb.add('John Jenkins','Advanced Microstuff','321-9942',

...'jjenkins@advmicro.com','disk drives')

ft. cdb.add('Fred Smith','Hitech Storage','332-1994',

... 'fredsmith@hitechstorage.com','magnetic tape')

ft. cdb.add('Al Watson',"Brains 'r Us",'335-2324',

...'al@brains.net','consulting')

ft. cdb.search('mary')

[Name: Mary Wilson
Company: Brainpower, Inc.
Phone: 222-3292
Email: mw@brainpower.net
Product: consulting]

ft. cdb[3] Name: Al Watson Company: Brains 'r Us Phone: 335-2324 Email: al@brains.net Product: consulting

10.8. INHERITANCE

161

ft. cdb['John Jenkins'] Name: John Jenkins Company: Advanced Microstuff Phone: 321-9942

Email: jjenkins@advmicro.com
Product: disk drives

All of the methods we implemented for the Frienddb class work correctly with our new class. Since we defined a Contact object, and explicitly defined an add method to use it, Python knows how to display the contacts properly.

Now suppose that we want to expand the search method to allow us to specify, using a keyword argument, whether we wish to search the database for a name, a company or a product. We've already developed a method to search for names when we wrote the Frienddb class, so we can use that when we're searching for names, and add additional code to handle the other cases. When you need to access a method from another class, you need to treat the method like a regular function. In other words, instead of following self with the method name, you call the function with self as the first argument to the method, as illustrated below when the search method from the Frienddb class is invoked in our new search method:

```
def search(self,name=",company=",product="):
results = []
if name:
found = Frienddb.search(self,name)
results.extend(found)
if company:
srch = re.compile(company,re.I)
found = []
for item in self.db:
if srch.search(item.company):
found.append(item)
results.extend(found)
if product:
srch = re.compile(product,re.I)
found = []
for item in self.db:
162 CHAPTER 10. WRITING MODULES
if srch.search(item.product):
```

```
found.append(item)
results.extend(found)
return results
```

(As in previous examples, this method would only make sense if it was part of the definition for the class Contactdb.) Now we can search for either names, companies or products:

```
ft. cdb = contactdb.Contactdb('new.db')

ft. found = cdb.search(product='consult')

ft. for i in found:

    ... print '-' * 10
    ... print i
    ...
    ----------
    Name: Mary Wilson
    Company: Brainpower, Inc.
    Phone: 222-3292
    Email: mw@brainpower.net
    Product: consulting
    ----------
    Name: Al Watson
    Company: Brains 'r Us
    Phone: 335-2324
    Email: al@brains.net
    Product: consulting

ft. found = cdb.search(name='mary')

ft. print found[0]

    Name: Mary Wilson
    Company: Brainpower, Inc.
    Phone: 222-3292
    Email: mw@brainpower.net
    Product: consulting
```

10.9. ADDING METHODS TO THE BASIC TYPES

163

10.9 Adding Methods to the Basic Types

While we started completely from scratch in designing methods and objects in the previous sections, many times the need for a new object can be met by simply adding one or two methods to an existing basic data type. To facilitate this, python provides the UserString, UserList and UserDict classes. These classes store a regular object in the data attribute, and allow you to quickly create new objects which have all the usual methods of a string, list or dictionary along with any new methods you care to define.

As an example, suppose we wish to create a dictionary that will "remem-ber" the order in which entries are added. Of course, this could be done by explicitly keeping a list of the keys, but would be awkward to implement because each time an entry was added to the dictionary, a separate state-ment would be needed to update the list.

By overloading the __setitem__ method, we can store each key as it is encountered; by providing a new method (say, okeys), we can retrieve the ordered list. To simplify matters, the __init__ method will not accept any arguments, so that the dictionary must be built incrementally. (When a dictionary is initialized in the usual way, the keys are added in a random order.) Here's an example of how such a dictionary could be implemented:

```
from UserDict import UserDict
class ODict(UserDict):
def __init__(self):
self._okeys = []
self.data = {}
def __setitem__(self,key,value):
self.data[key] = value
if key not in self._okeys:
self._okeys.append(key)
def okeys(self):
return self._okeys
```

After creating an object of type ODict, we can manipulate it just as any other dictionary, since, when you invoke an existing method, the UserDict class knows to operate on the data attribute of the object. However, the

164 CHAPTER 10. WRITING MODULES

new okeys method is available to provide the keys in the order in which they were created:

```
ft. from odict import ODict

ft. mydict = ODict()

ft. words = ['cat','dog','duck','chicken','goat']

ft. for w in words:

... mydict[w] = len(w)
...
>>> mydict.keys()
['goat', 'chicken', 'duck', 'dog', 'cat']
>>> mydict.okeys()
['cat', 'dog', 'duck', 'chicken', 'goat']
```

10.10 Iterators

Now suppose that we'd like to be able to iterate over the keys of our ODict object using a for loop, with the keys presented in the order in which they were added. To acheive this goal, we need to define an __iter__ method which simply returns itself, and a next method to return the keys in the order we desire. When you implement an iterator, it's your responsibility to raise a StopIteration exception when the items of your object are exhausted. Furthermore, you'll usually need to define a new attribute in your object to help you keep track of the most recently returned element. In this example, you'd need to set the self.count variable to 0 in the __iter__ method. The other additions which are required are shown below:

```
def iter(self):
self.count = 0
return(self)
def next:
if self.count >= len(self._okeys):
raise StopIteration
```

```
rval = self._okeys[self.count]
self.count = self.count + 1
return(rval)
```

Python I/O

Python supports I/O operations like input and output operations which are specifically called file operations. It will provide basic idea regarding the file operations like how to open a file, reading and writing to files, close a file etc.

What is the benefit?

Imagine, storing volatile data after completion of work which lose every time when you close your Computer, or the program ends. So, we need files to save data permanently which we can make use of in future. That is why file handling is important.

Take an example, you have created a CGPA calculator program in which you can calculate the CGPA of students by calculating the marks in 5 different subjects. If you will get 400 students' marks to calculate CGPA, then will you try to take input of all students by manually feeding the inputs one by one? Quite hectic, Right? Here come the file operations for rescue in which you can simply store the 400 students list and marks in a text file or CSV file and can access all the data at a time by simply accessing it using Python's built-in I/O functions.

How Python helps in file handling?

Unlike of other programming languages like C, C++ where we need separate headers file like "fstream" or in java importing "java.io" package, we do not need anything specific to import or add in python file as I/O tools are built-in part of the language environment itself. So, it is more convenient to use.

Types of Files in Python:

We need to deal with basically two types of files in Python:

1. Text file
2. Binary file

1.Text File:

The text file is a normal file which you create using a notepad or editor in your system which contains some lines of text which does not contain any specific encoding. For Ex: .txt file containing some texts.

2.Binary file:

- The file with which we deal every day, are all binary files starting from image, audio files to .doc , .xls , .pdf files which contain data in binary format.
- These files need special handlings as they require specific software to open. For Ex: Image viewer for opening a .jpg file.

Basic Operations in Python I/O:

There are basically three different types of file operations involved in Python I/O which are:

1. Open a file.
2. Perform read and write operation.
3. Close a file.

1. **Open a file in python:**

Before accessing a file, the foremost thing to do is opening a file for which python has the built-in function *open()*to open the respective file.

Syntax:

f = open(filename, mode)

Note: Instead of file name, you can also provide the *file-path* for opening the file in above syntax.

The open() returns a file object which contains some predefined methods to work with file operations like reading or writing in file. So we need to open a file first in order to read and write as the file object provides all methods.

Properties of Open():

Let's take an example of open() for better understanding:

Arrow Arrow Arrow

Up withUp withUp with

solid fill solid fill solid fill *f = open("sample.text","r")*

(file object) (file name) (mode)

As mentioned in above syntax open() should contain:

1. **File object attributes**:

The file object attribute contains all related information about the file which we open using open(). It provides various attributes to extract information related the file like:

- **f.name :**It returns the name of the opened file.
- **f.mode :**It returns the mode of the file in which it opens.
- **f.closed:** It is to check whether a file is closed or not. If it is closed, will return true else return false.

Text Description automatically generated with medium confidence

2. **filename:** The filename mentioned is the source file which you

want to work with which present in current directory.

Ex: "sample.txt" #location-current directory

Note: Instead of file name you can provide relative path to the working directory.

For Ex:

Arrow

Up with

solid fill *f=open("C:/Python38/sample.txt")*

Path address of file present

In Python38 directory

3. **Mode:**

Mode is another property of open() which is used to specify what we want to do in the file which we are accessing. Different types of mode specifiers are available:

- **"r"– read only mode(default mode):** This mode is used to read the file only , not to make any changes to it. It is the default mode when opening a file.

Ex:

f = open("sample.txt" , "r")
We can also skip the mode specifier in the syntax if we only need read access as it will consider as default.
Ex:
f = open("sample.txt") #provide read access

- **"w"-write mode:** This mode is used when we want to make some changes to the file like writing in the file or alter the file which replacesall the previous data and create a new one with new contents changed by us. Overwrites the file if the file exists. If the file does not exist, creates a new file for writing.

  Ex:
  f = open("sample.txt", "w")

- **"a"- append mode:** This mode is used to append some lines in the file by adding new lines at the end of the file as the file pointer in this mode presents at the end of the file.If the file does not exist, it creates a new file for writing.

  Ex:
  f = open("sample.txt","a")

- **'r+' – Read/Write Mode**: This mode is used to read the file and write into the file as well.

- **'w+' – Read/Write Mode**: This mode is used to write and read in file which overwrites the file by replacing the old contents with new one written by us and create a new file if the file does not exist.

- **'a+' – Append and Read Mode**: This mode allows us to append data at the end of the file as well as to read the information of the file. The file pointer presents at the end of the file to append data. It creates a new file if it does not exist.

Handling different file types:
Text files:

In the above mentioned examples, we have mentioned how to deal with text files exclusively which is the default type in the open().

But you can also add another specifier "t" in order to specify the text file which is default, so unnecessary to use to avoid conflict.

- **"t"-Read/Write as text mode**(default)

Binary files:

Handling the binary files are just same as the text files by specifying the modes. The only difference is, we need to mention the type of file by "b" which is binary.

- **"rb"**- Read in binary mode
- **"wb"**- Write in binary mode
- **"ab"**- Append in binary mode
- **"r+b"**- Read and Write in binary mode
- **"w+b"**- Write and Read in binary mode
- **"a+b"**- Append and Read in binary mode

Ex:

Arrow Arrow
Up withUp with
solid fill solid fill *f = open("image.jpg", "rb")*
(Binary file) (read in binary mode)

Close a file in python:

After completion of operations in file, it is a good practice to properly close the file as:

- it will release all the resources used by the program by cleaning the buffer
- frees up the memory.

After closing the file, the data successfully stores in the volatile memory and all other buffer data flush out. The syntax for closing the file is by using the file object created by open() which calls the function close(). For Ex:

file-obj.close()

After successfully closing the file, if you will further try to perform any operations like reading or writing on it, it will show ValueError.

Text Description automatically generated

Python with keyword:

It is a good practice to use with keyword during file handling as if any kind of exception or error occurs, it will close the file automatically. Even same will happen when break or return or statements inside with block execute successfully . So we don't need to explicitly call close().

A screenshot of a computer Description automatically generated with medium confidence

Here in the above code snippet sample.txt closed automatically by printing the data.

Read and Write operations in a file:

Before reading and writing the file, it must be needed to be opened first. So the file must be opened using the respective modes in order to access the read and write operations.

Read to a file:

The file should be opened with "r" mode to perform the read operation.

Python I/O

1. **Introduction:**

Python supports I/O operations like input and output operations which are specifically called file operations. It will provide basic idea regarding the file operations like how to open a file, reading and writing to files, close a file etc.

2. **What is the benefit?**

Imagine, storing volatile data after completion of work which lose every time when you close your Computer, or the program ends. So, we need files to save data permanently which we can make use of in future. That is why file handling is important.

Take an example, you have created a CGPA calculator program in which you can calculate the CGPA of students by calculating the marks in 5 different subjects. If you will get 400 students' marks to calculate CGPA, then will you try to take input of all students by manually feeding the inputs one by one? Quite hectic, Right? Here come the file operations for rescue in which you can simply store the 400 students list and marks in a text file or CSV file and can access all the data at a time by simply accessing it using Python's built-in I/O functions.

3. **How Python helps in file handling?**

Unlike of other programming languages like C, C++ where we need separate headers file like "fstream" or in java importing "java.io" package, we do not need anything specific to import or add in python file as I/O tools are built-in part of the language environment itself. So, it is more convenient to use.

4. **Types of Files in Python:**

We need to deal with basically two types of files in Python:

A. Text file
B. Binary file

A. **Text File:**

The text file is a normal file which you create using a notepad or editor in your system which contains some lines of text which does not contain any specific encoding. For Ex: *.txt* file containing some texts.

B. **Binary file:**

- The file with which we deal every day, are all binary files starting from *image, audio* files to *.doc , .xls , .pdf* files which contain data in binary format.

- These files need special handlings as they require specific software to open. For Ex: Image viewer for opening a .jpg file.

5. **Basic Operations in Python I/O:**

There are basically three different types of file operations involved in Python I/O which are:

1. Open a file.
2. Perform read and write operation.
3. Close a file.

   1. **Open a file in python:**

Before accessing a file, the foremost thing to do is opening a file for which python has the built-in function *open()*to open the respective file.

Syntax:

f = open(filename, mode)

Note: Instead of file name, you can also provide the *file-path* for opening the file in above syntax.

The *open()* returns a file object which contains some predefined methods to work with file operations like reading or writing in file. So, we need to open a file first in order to read and write as the file object provides all methods.

1. **Properties of Open():**

Let's take an example of *open()* for better understanding:
f = open("sample.text", "r")
(file object) (file name) (mode)
As mentioned in above syntax *open()* should contain:

1. **file object attributes**:

The file object attribute contains all related information about the file which we open using *open().* It provides various attributes to extract information related the file like:

- **f.name :** It returns the name of the opened file.
- **f.mode :** It returns the mode of the file in which it opens.
- **f.closed :** It is to check whether a file is closed or not. If it is closed, will return true else return false.

2. **filename:** The filename mentioned is the source file which

you want to work with which present in current directory.
Ex: *"sample.txt"* #location-current directory
Note: Instead of file name you can provide relative path to the working directory.
For Ex:
f =open("C:/Python38/sample.txt")
Path address of file present
In Python38 directory

3. **Mode:**

Mode is another property of *open()* which is used to specify what we want to do in the file which we are accessing. Different types of mode specifiers are available:

- **"r" – read only mode(default mode):** This mode is used to read the file only , not to make any changes to it. It is the default mode when opening a file.

  Ex:
  f = open("sample.txt", "r")
  We can also skip the mode specifier in the syntax if we only need
  read access as it will consider as default.
  Ex:
  f = open("sample.txt") #provide read access

- **"w"-write mode:** This mode is used when we want to make some changes to the file like writing in the file or alter the file which replaces all the previous data and create a new one with new contents changed by us. Overwrites the file if the file exists. If the file does not exist, creates a new file for writing.

Ex:
f = open("sample.txt", "w")

- **"a"- append mode:** This mode is used to append some lines in the file by adding new lines at the end of the file as the file pointer in this mode presents at the end of the file. If the file does not exist, it creates a new file for writing.

  Ex:
  f = open("sample.txt" , "a")

- **'r+' – Read/Write Mode**: This mode is used to read the file and write into the file as well.

- **'w+' – Read/Write Mode**: This mode is used to write and read in file which overwrites the file by replacing the old contents with new one written by us and create a new file if the file does not exist.

- **'a+' – Append and Read Mode**: This mode allows us to append data at the end of the file as well as to read the information of the file. The file pointer presents at the end of the file to append data. It creates a new file if it does not exist.

2. **Handling different file types:**

1. **Text files:**

In the above mentioned examples, we have mentioned how to deal with text files exclusively which is the default type in the *open()*.

But you can also add another specifier "t" in order to specify the text file, which is default, so unnecessary to use to avoid conflict.

- **"t"-Read/Write as text mode**(default)

2. **Binary files:**

Handling the binary files are just same as the text files by specifying the modes. The only difference is, we need to mention the type of file by "b" which is binary.

- **"rb"**- Read in binary mode
- **"wb"**- Write in binary mode
- **"ab"**- Append in binary mode
- **"r+b"**- Read and Write in binary mode
- **"w+b"**- Write and Read in binary mode
- **"a+b"**- Append and Read in binary mode

Ex:
f = open("image.jpg" , "rb")
(Binary file) (read in binary mode)

2. **Close a file in python:**

After completion of operations in file, it is a good practice to properly close the file as:

- it will release all the resources used by the program by cleaning the buffer.
- frees up the memory.

After closing the file, the data successfully stores in the volatile memory and all other buffer data flush out. The syntax for closing the file is by using the file object created by *open()* which calls the function close().

For Ex:

f.close()

After successfully closing the file, if you will further try to perform any operations like reading or writing on it, it will show *ValueError*.

1. **Python with keyword:**

It is a good practice to use with keyword during file handling as if any kind of exception or error occurs, it will close the file automatically. Even same will happen when break or return or statements inside with block execute successfully. So we don't need to explicitly call *close()*.

Here in the above code snippet sample.txt has closed automatically by printing the data. That's why *f.closed* has given *true* as the file is closed.

3. **Read and Write operations in a file:**

Before reading and writing the file, it must be needed to be opened first. So, the file must be opened using the respective modes in order to access the read and write operations.

1. **Read to a file:**

The file should be opened with "r" mode to perform the read operation. The file object has already been created during the opening of the file. This file object provides different methods to perform various reading operations like:

read():

- The *read()* is used to read the contents of the file which returns some *string value* in case of text file and *bytes object* in case of binary files.

Ex: *f.read()*

- We can also provide *size* parameter in this method by specifying the size of the string to be printed.

Ex: *f.read(4)* #4 is the size

- At the end of the file, the *size()* returns *single quote*(' ')specifying the empty string.

readline():

This method is used to read the file line by line, reading one line at a time where at the end of each line '\n' is printed showing the end of the line.

For Ex: *f.readline()*

Note: You can also loop over the file object to extract all the lines which is memory efficient, much simpler and faster as compared printing every line one by one.

readlines():

This method returns a list of all lines in the file.

2. **Write to a file:**

- In order to write into a file, it must be needed to open the file in "w" or "a" mode where we can write and append new contents in the file.
- *write()* is used to add string values in text file and bytes object in binary files.
- For Ex: *f.write("Hello Payal")* #string "Hello Payal" is written to the file
- *write()* returns the no of characters written to the file. In the above example, we have opened a binary file "image.jpg" and written some byte codes into the file which has returned 16 as no of characters.

Note: In "w" and "a" mode, if the file does not exist, it creates a new one and writes into the file.

3. **Some other file object methods:**

- **tell():** This method returns the file object's current position which is in no of bytes from the beginning of the file.

  Ex: *f.tell()*

- **seek(byte value):** This method moves the pointer to the location which byte number is given as parameter in the method.

  Ex: *f.seek(4)*

6. **Example of Python I/O:**

Let's try out the above-mentioned problem of calculating the Student grades from mark in section 2. Some student names and their marks in different subjects have taken in csv file named "studentmarks.csv". Here instead of read() and write() function, the built-in csv package is used to read and write data from csv file which is more efficient and faster.

CSV File:

Source Code:

The Possible output of the above code:

It is giving the name of the students along with the grades calculated. We can also write the student data into the csv file and calculate his/her grade as well.

Complex Datatype

Before getting into a Complex datatype we must need to know what is a complex number? As we studied in math, a complex number is a combination of both the Real component and the imaginary component like 5+6i, Where 5 is the real component and 6 multiplied by 'i' is the Imaginary component. Likewise, the complex data type in python is represented as " a + bj"(a=Real component, b Multiply by 'j' imaginary component).

Ex: a = 6 + 8j

Print(type(a))

OutPut: <Class 'complex'>

According to math j is defind by

So j=√-1

In python, you must use 'j' or 'J' as in the imaginary part. Use of Any other character will throw a syntax error. If you give 'J' as input by default python always return complex number with small 'j' in output.

Ex: a=2 + 3J

Print(a)

Output: 2 + 3j

Ex: a = 2 + 3i

Print(a)

Out put: SyntaxError: invalid syntax

If you want to access only the real and imaginary value from a complex number you can do that by .real and .imag variable. It always returns a floating-point value as an output.

Ex. a= 2 + 3J

print(a.real) //access real part

print(a.imag) // access imaginary part

Output: 2.0

3.0

Note: While working on complex data type in the real part you can assign any type of number(decimal, binary, octal, hexadecimal) but in the case of the imaginary part, you must assign a decimal number. Another type will through error.

Ex: a=2.4 + 3.5j // dec imal number in both the part

b= 0B1111 + 20j //Binary number in real and int in imaginary part

print(a)

Print(b)

Output: (2.4 + 3.5j)

(15 + 20j)

Ex: a=2.4 + 0B1111j //binary number in imaginary part

print(a)

Output: SyntaxError: invalid syntax

Variousc operation in complex data type

You can perform various arithmatic operation by using complex data type.

Ex: a = 2.5 + 6j

b = 2 + 3.2j

print(a+b) //Addition

print(a-b) //Substraction

print(a*b) //Multiplication

print(a/b) //Division

Output: (4.5+9.2j)

(0.5+2.8j)

(-14.200000000000003+20j)

(1.699438202247191 + 0.28089887640449435j)

By using complex() method you can convert any number or string into a complex number. This method takes two parameters and returns a complex number. The first parameter is real and the second one is the imaginary part. If you are providing only one parameter it will take that as a real part. If you provide no arguments by default it will return '0j'as an output

Ex. a=complex(1) // Single parameter

b = coplex(2.3,5.3) //Two parameter

c = (complex()) //No argument

print(a)

print(b)

print(c)

Output: (1+0j)

(2.3 + 5.3j)

0j

In the case of a string, It allows only one string parameter. If the first argument is a string type, it does not allow any other second parameter. Providing a second argument will raise an error.

Ex: a = complex('2.444')

print(a)

Output: (2.444+0j)

Ex: a= complex('1',2)

print(a)

Output: TypeError

SET

A set is an unordered collection of items, where the items of the set must be unique(No duplication) and immutable(Items can't be changed but can add new items). Unordered means, the items of the set will appear in different sequence every time you run the program. Set items can't be accessed by index or key.

There are several ways to create a set; The simple one is to enclose the elements in curly brackets separated by a comma "{}". The second one is by using the "set()" build-in function. It can have any items and they may be different data types(int,float,string,tuple etc.) except dictionaries and set itself.

Ex. Num = {4,1,2,3,4,5,4} } //Set of integers

print(Num)

Output: {1,2,3,4,5}

Ex. City = {"Delhi", "Kolkata", "Mumbai", "Bhubaneswar"} //Set of Strings

print(City)

Output: { "Kolkata", "Bhubaneswar" ,"Mumbai", "Delhi"}

Ex. Mix_set = {1.5, (3,5,6) , "IIT"} //Set of mix datatype

Print(Mix_set)

Output: {1.5,"IIT",(3,5,6)}

Creation of set by set() build-in-function:

Ex: my_set=set((1,2, "IIT", "NIT", 8.5))

print("my_set")

Output: {'IIT',2,8.5, 'NIT',1}

Accessing Items from Set

You can't access items from a set by using indexing. For access items from set you need to use for loop.

Ex: my_set={"Delhi", "Kolkata", "Mumbai", "Bhubaneswar"}

for i in my_set:

print(i)

Output: Kolkata

Bhubaneswar

Delhi

Mumbai

For checking an item is present or not you can use 'in' keyword. If the searchable item will be present in the set, python will show the output as a boolean value "True" else "False".

Ex: my_set={"Delhi", "Kolkata", "Mumbai", "Bhubaneswar"}

print("Patna" in my_set)

Output: False

Modifying set in python

Once the set is created you can't change the items but you can add new items to it. For adding a single item **add()** method is used.

Ex. my_set={"Delhi", "Kolkata", "Mumbai", "Bhubaneswar"}

my_set.add("pune")

Print(my_set)
Output: Kolkata
Bhubaneswar
Delhi
Mumbai
Pune

update() method is used toadd multiple elements to the set. It can take any iterable objects like lists, tuples, string, set etc. and update the base set.

Ex: my_set={"Delhi", "Kolkata", "Mumbai", "Bhubaneswar"}
my_set.update(['Bangalore','chennai'])
print(my_set)
Output: Kolkata
Bhubaneswar
Delhi
Mumbai
Bangalore
chennai

Removing items from set

To remove any particular item from a set **remove()** and **discard()** method is used. The only difference between the two is that, if any item is present **remove()** method removes that item, if not it raises a key error message but in **discard()** method leaves a set without error if the item is not present.

Ex. my_set={"Delhi", "Kolkata", "Mumbai", "Bhubaneswar"}
my_set.remove('Mumbai')
print(my_set)
Output: Kolkata
Bhubaneswar
Delhi

Ex. my_set={"Delhi", "Kolkata", "Mumbai", "Bhubaneswar"}
my_set.remove('Chennai')
print(my_set)
Output: KeyError('Chennai')

There is one more build-in method pop() which also can remove items from a set. As you studied in other language pop() removes the last element but as set is an unordered datatype you never know which item will get removed by pop() from the set. That is completely arbitrary.

Ex. my_set={"Delhi", "Kolkata", "Mumbai", "Bhubaneswar"}
X = my_set.pop()
print(X) //removed item
Output: Delhi

We can remove all the items from a set by using **clear()** method and to delete the set completely we use **del()** method

Ex. my_set={"Delhi", "Kolkata", "Mumbai", "Bhubaneswar"}
my_set.clear()
print(my_set)
Output: set()

Join operations

Set is used for performing mathematics set operations such as union, intersection, difference, and symmetric difference.

Union operation

Mathematically union of set A and B means a combination of all the elements from set A and set B. Likewise, the same concept is followed by python as well. So for performing union operation in python we use union() build-in method or by using "|" operator we can perform the same.

Ex:
```
A= {1,2,3,4}
B= {3,4,5,6}
print(A.union(B))
Output: {1,2,3,4,5,6}
```
Ex:
```
A= {1,2,3,4}
B= {3,4,5,6}
print(A | B)
Output: {1,2,3,4,5,6}
```
Intersection operation

Likewise in math intersection of set A and set B means all the common elements of both the set. For performing this operation python has build-in method intersection(). With the help of "&" operator, the same operation can be performed.

Ex:
```
A= {1,2,3,4}
B= {3,4,5,6}
print(A.intersection(B))
Output: {3,4}
```
Ex:
```
A= {1,2,3,4}
B= {3,4,5,6}
print(A & B)
Output: {3,4}
```
Set diffrence

The difference of set A from set B means(A - B) a set of element those are only present in set A not in B and difference of set B from set A means(B - A) the only the elements of B. To perform the above operation python has **difference()** build-in method and by "-" operator can perform the same.

Ex: **A difference B**
```
A= {1,2,3,4}
B= {3,4,5,6}
print(A - B)
Output: {1,2}
```
Ex: **B difference A**
```
A= {1,2,3,4}
B= {3,4,5,6}
print(B.difference(A))
Output: {5,6}
```
Symmentric difference

Symmetric difference of set A and B means, all the elements from both the set except the mutual elements of both the set.It can be performed by symmentric_diffrence() method or by "^" operator.

Ex:
```
A= {1,2,3,4}
B= {3,4,5,6}
print(A ^ B)
```

Output: {1,2,5,6}
Ex:
A= {1,2,3,4}
B= {3,4,5,6}
print(A.symmentric_difference(B))
Output: {1,2,5,6}

Dictionary

Dictionary is an unordered, mutable collection of items. Each item of the dictionary has a key and value(key: value) pair enclosed in curly braces "{ }" and separated by commas. The keys must be unique and immutable type(number, string, etc.) and the values for any corresponding keys can be of any type. There is no problem if the values are repeating. But the dictionaries can't have two items for the same key.

Creating a dictionary

We can create a dictionary by using "{}" and by using the **dict()** built-in function.

Ex: my_dict = {} //Empty dictionary
Ex: my_dict = {1: " School", 2: "college"} //dictionary with int key
Ex: my_dict = {"college": "IIT",
"Name" : "Avijit",
"Marks" : [90,88.95]} //dictionary with mixed key
Output: {'college' : 'IIT', 'Name' : 'Avijit', 'Marks' : [90,88,95]}
Creating dictinaries by **dict():**
Ex: my_dict = dict({'college' : 'IIT', 'Name' : 'Avijit', 'Marks' : [90,88,95]})
Output: {'college' : 'IIT', 'Name' : 'Avijit', 'Marks' : [90,88,95]}

Accessing elements

We use index values in another data type like list, tuple, and string for accessing elements but in a dictionary, we use the keys to access. There are two ways to access items from the dictionary by keys. The first one is by square brackets [ ] and the second one is by get( ) method.

If the searchable key is not present in dictionary usees of square bracket [ ] will through a KeyError but in other side use of get() will return None if the key is missing.

Ex: my_dict = {"college": "IIT",
"Name" : "Avijit",
"Marks" : [90,88.95]}
print(my_dict['college'])
print(my_dict.get('Marks')
Output: IIT
[90, 88, 95]
Ex: my_dict = {"college": "IIT",
"Name" : "Avijit",
"Marks" : [90,88,95]}
print(my_dict['Address'])
print(my_dict.get('Address'))
Output: KeyError : 'Address'
None

To access only keys and values from dictionary keys() & values() method you can use. keys() will return a list of all the key and value() will all the values of a specific dictionary.

Ex: my_dict = {"college": "IIT",
"Name" : "Avijit",
"Marks" : [90,88,95]}
print(my_dict.keys())

print(my_dict.values())
Output. dict_keys(['college', 'Name', 'Marks'])
dict_values(['IIT', 'Avijit', [90 ,88,95]])
You can search a key is present in a dictionary or not by using 'in' keyword.
Ex: my_dict = {"college": "IIT",
"Name" : "Avijit",
"Marks" : [90,88,95]}
If 'Name' in my_dict:
Print("Yes, that is here")

Adding and Changing elements

As we know the dictionary is mutable in nature, so we can perform add and change operations to it by referring to its key name or can do by update() method.

Ex: my_dict = {"college": "IIT",
"Name" : "Avijit",
"Marks" : [90,88,95]}
My_dict['Marks'] = [99,98,95]
print(my_dict)
Output: {'college' : 'IIT', 'Name' : 'Avijit', 'Marks' : [99,98,95]}
Ex: my_dict = {"college": "IIT",
"Name" : "Avijit",
"Marks" : [90,88,95]}
My_dict.update({'college': 'IITKGP'})
print(my_dict)
Output: {'college' : 'IITKGP', 'Name' : 'Avijit', 'Marks' : [90,98,95]}
By the help of **update()** methodandassignment operator we can add new item to dictionary.
Ex: my_dict = {"college": "IIT",
"Name" : "Avijit",
"Marks" : [90,88,95]}
my_dict['Year']=2021
my_dict.update({'Branch': 'CSE'})
print(my_dict)
Output: {'college' : 'IIT', 'Name' : 'Avijit', 'Marks' : [90,98,95],'Year' : 2021,'Branch' : 'CSE'}

Removing elemets

Likewise, Set there are several methods to perform remove operation from the dictionary. pop() method is used to remove a particular item by providing a key. It returns deleted key value. popitem() method removes last element(key : value) of the dictionary from the dictionary.

Ex: my_dict = {"college": "IIT",
"Name" : "Avijit",
"Marks" : [90,88,95],
"Branch" : "CSE"}
print(my_dict.pop('Marks'))
print(my_dict.popitem())
print(my_dict)
Output: [90 , 88 , 95]
('Branch', 'CSE')
{'college':'IIT', 'Name':'Avijit'}
clear() is use for remove all elemets from dictionary at once,It returns None. del() for delete the entire dictionary.
Ex: my_dict = {"college": "IIT",

"Name" : "Avijit",
"Marks" : [90,88,95],
"Branch" : "CSE"}
print(my_dict.clear())
Output: None

Cross Validation Techniques in Machine Learning

There is always importance of validating the stability of the current machine learning model. Sometimes the ML approach can't fit the model to the training data and we hope it would accurately work for the real data it has never been tested before.

Cross-validation technique can be used for evaluating ML models by training models based on subsets of the input data and evaluating on the complementary subset of the input data. In k-fold **cross-validation**, we can split the input data into k subsets of data also called as folds.

In machine learning process , some cases we cannot fit the model on the training data and can't say that the model will work accurately for the real data. To overcome this, we must timely assess that our model is able to capture the correct patterns from the data, too much noise in data is skipped. So we need assurance that our model is low on bias and variance.

Cross-Validation Process

Cross-validation is a process in which users train the model utilising the subset of the data-set and then evaluate the same using the complementary subset of the data-set.

The three major steps involved in cross-validation are as follows :

1. First Reserve some subset of sample data set.
2. Utilise the rest data set to train the model.
3. Validate or Test the model using the reserved subset of the data-set and find out accuracy .

Methods of Cross Validation

Validation Method:

In Validation method, users perform training on the half of the data i.e. 50% of the given data-set and rest 50% is consumed for the training purpose. The major drawback of this method is that we perform training on the 50% of the dataset, it can be possible that the remaining 50% of the data contains some important information which we are leaving while training our model i.e higer bias.

LOOCV (Leave One Out Cross Validation)

In this method, we perform training on the whole data-set but leaves only one data-point of the available data-set and then iterates for each data-point. It has some advantages as well as disadvantages also.

An advantage of using this method is that we make use of all data points and hence it is low bias.

The major drawback of this method is that it leads to higher variation in the testing model as we are testing against one data point. If the data point is an outlier it can lead to higher variation. Another drawback is it takes a lot of execution time as it iterates over 'the number of data points' times.

K-Fold Cross Validation

In this method, we split the data-set into k number of subsets(known as folds) then we perform training on the all the subsets but leave one(k-1) subset for the evaluation of the trained model. In this method, we iterate k times with a different subset reserved for testing purpose each time.

Note:

It is always suggested that the value of k should be 10 as the lower value
of k is takes towards validation and higher value of k leads to LOOCV method.

Example

The diagram below shows an example of the training subsets and evaluation subsets generated in k-fold cross-validation. Here, we have total 25 instances. In first iteration we use the first 20 percent of data for evaluation, and the remaining 80 percent for training([1-5] testing and [5-25] training) while in the second iteration we use the second subset of 20 percent for evaluation, and the remaining three subsets of the data for training([5-10] testing and [1-5 and 10-25] training), and so on.

Total instances: 25

Value of k : 5

No. Iteration Training set observations Testing set observations

1 [5 6 7 8 9 10 11 12 13 14 15 16 17 18 19 20 21 22 23 24] [0 1 2 3 4]

2 [0 1 2 3 4 10 11 12 13 14 15 16 17 18 19 20 21 22 23 24] [5 6 7 8 9]

3 [0 1 2 3 4 5 6 7 8 9 15 16 17 18 19 20 21 22 23 24] [10 11 12 13 14]

4 [0 1 2 3 4 5 6 7 8 9 10 11 12 13 14 20 21 22 23 24] [15 16 17 18 19]

5 [0 1 2 3 4 5 6 7 8 9 10 11 12 13 14 15 16 17 18 19] [20 21 22 23 24]

Comparision of train/test split to cross-validation

Advantages of train/test split:

1. This runs K times faster than K-fold cross-validation because K-fold cross-validation repeats the train/test split K-times.

2. Simpler to examine the detailed results of the testing process.

Advantages of cross-validation:

1. More accurate estimate of out-of-sample accuracy.

2. More "efficient" use of data as every observation is used for both training and testing.

Python code for k fold cross-validation.

```
# This code may not be run on GFG IDE
# as required packages are not found.
# importing cross-validation from sklearn package.
from sklearn import cross_validation
# value of K is 10.
data = cross_validation.KFold(len(train_set), n_folds=10, indices=False)
```

Cross-Validation in Machine Learning

Validation

*This process of deciding whether the numerical results quantifying hypothesized relationships between variables, are acceptable as descriptions of the data, is known as **validation**.* Generally, an error estimation for the model is made after training, better known as evaluation of residuals. In this process, a numerical estimate of the difference in predicted and original responses is done, also called the training error. However, *this only gives us an idea about how well our model does on data used to train it.* Now its possible that the model is underfitting or overfitting the data. So, the ***problem with this evaluation technique is that it does not give an indication of how well the learner will generalize to an independent/ unseen data set.*** **Getting this idea about our model is known as Cross Validation.**

Holdout Method

Now a *basic remedy for this involves removing a part of the training data and using it to get predictions from the model trained on rest of the data.* The error estimation then tells how our model is doing on unseen data or the validation set. **This is a simple kind of cross validation technique, also known as the holdout method**. Although this method doesn't take any overhead to compute and is better than traditional validation, ***it still suffers from issues of high variance. This is because it is not certain which data points will end up in the validation set and the result might be entirely different for different sets.***

Then when training is **done**, the data that was removed can be used to test the performance of the learned model on ``new'' data. This is the basic idea for a whole class of model evaluation methods called **cross validation**. The holdout method is the simplest kind of **cross validation.**

K-Fold Cross Validation

As there is never enough data to train your model, *removing a part of it for validation poses a problem of underfitting.* ***By reducing the training data, we risk losing important patterns/ trends in data set, which in turn increases error induced by bias.*** So, what we require is a method that provides ample data for training the model and also leaves ample data for validation. K Fold cross validation does exactly that.

In **K Fold cross validation**, the data is divided into k subsets. Now the holdout method is repeated k times, such that ***each time, one of the k subsets is used as the test set/ validation set and the other k-1 subsets are put together to form a training set.*** The *error estimation is averaged over all k trials to get total effectiveness of our model.* As can be seen, every data point gets to be in a validation set exactly once, and gets to be in a training set *k-1*times. ***This significantly reduces bias as we are using most of the data for fitting, and also significantly reduces variance as most of the data is also being used in validation set.*** Interchanging the training and test sets also adds to the effectiveness of this method. **As a general rule and empirical evidence, K = 5 or 10 is generally preferred**, but nothing's fixed and it can take any value.

Stratified K-Fold Cross Validation

In some cases, there may be a large imbalance in the response variables. For example, in dataset concerning price of houses, there might be large number of houses having high price. Or in case of classification, there might be several times more negative samples than positive samples. For such problems, ***a slight variation in the K Fold cross validation technique is made, such that each fold contains approximately the same percentage of samples of each target class as the complete set, or in case of prediction problems, the mean response value is approximately equal in all the folds.*** This variation is also known as **Stratified K Fold**.

Above explained validation techniques are also referred to as Non-exhaustive cross validation methods.These do not compute all ways of splitting the original sample, i.e. you just have to decide how many subsets need to be made. Also, these are approximations of ***method explained below, also called Exhaustive Methods, that computes all possible ways the data can be split into training and test sets.***

Leave-P-Out Cross Validation

This approach leaves p data points out of training data, i.e. if there are n data points in the original sample then, n-p samples are used to train the model and p points are used as the validation set. This is repeated for all combinations in which original sample can be separated this way, and then the error is averaged for all trials, to give overall effectiveness.

This method is exhaustive in the sense that it needs to train and validate the model for all possible combinations, and for moderately large p, it can become computationally infeasible.

A particular case of this method is when p = 1. This is known as Leave one out cross validation. This method is generally preferred over the previous one because ***it does not suffer from the intensive computation, as number of possible combinations is equal to number of data points in original sample or n.***

Cross Validation is ***a very useful technique for assessing the effectiveness of your model, particularly in cases where you need to mitigate overfitting.*** It is ***also of use in determining the hyper parameters of your model***, in the sense that which parameters will result in lowest test error. This is all the basic you need to get started with cross validation. You can get started with all kinds of validation techniques using **Scikit-Learn**, that gets you up and running with just a few lines of code in python.

1. Why do models lose stability?
2. What is cross validation?
3. A few common methods used for cross validation

    - The Validation set Approach
    - Leave out one cross validation (LOOCV)
    - k-fold cross validation
    - Stratified k-fold cross validation
    - Adversarial validation
    - Cross validation for time series
    - Custom cross validation techniques

4. How to measure the model's bias-variance?

Why do models lose stability?

Let's understand this using the below snapshot illustrating the fit of various models:

Here, we are trying to find the relationship between size and price. To achieve this, we have taken the following steps:

1. We've established the relationship using a linear equation for which the plots have been shown. The first plot has a high error from training data points. Therefore, this will not perform well on either public or the private leaderboard. This is an example of **"Underfitting".** In this case, our model fails to capture the underlying trend of the data
2. In the second plot, we just found the right relationship between price and size, i.e., low training error and generalization of the relationship
3. In the third plot, we found a relationship which has almost zero training error. This is because the relationship is developed by considering each deviation in the data point (including noise), i.e., the model is too sensitive and captures random patterns which are present only in the current dataset. This is an example of **"Overfitting"**. In this relationship, there could be a high deviation between the public and private leaderboards

A common practice in data science competitions is to iterate over various models to find a better performing model. However, it becomes difficult to distinguish whether this improvement in score is coming because we are capturing the relationship better, or we are just over-fitting the data. To find the right answer for this question, we use validation techniques. This method helps us in achieving more generalized relationships.

What is Cross Validation?

Cross Validation is a technique which involves reserving a particular sample of a dataset on which you do not train the model. Later, you test your model on this sample before finalizing it.

Here are the steps involved in cross validation:

1. You *reserve* a sample data set
2. Train the model using the remaining part of the dataset
3. Use the reserve sample of the test (validation) set. This will help you in gauging the effectiveness of your model's performance. If your model delivers a positive result on validation data, go ahead with the current model. It rocks!

A few common methods used for Cross Validation

There are various methods available for performing cross validation. I've discussed a few of them in this section.

The validation set approach

In this approach, we reserve 50% of the dataset for validation and the remaining 50% for model training. However, a major disadvantage of this approach is that since we are training a model on only 50% of the dataset, there is a huge possibility that we might miss out on some interesting information about the data which will lead to a higher bias.

Python Code:

```
train, validation = train_test_split(data, test_size=0.50, random_state = 5)
```

R Code:

```
set.seed(101) # Set Seed so that same sample can be reproduced in future also
# Now Selecting 50% of data as sample from total 'n' rows of the data
sample <- sample.int(n = nrow(data), size = floor(.50*nrow(data)), replace = F)
train <- data[sample, ]
test <- data[-sample, ]
```

Leave one out cross validation (LOOCV)

In this approach, we reserve only one data point from the available dataset, and train the model on the rest of the data. This process iterates for each data point. This also has its own advantages and disadvantages. Let's look at them:

- We make use of all data points, hence the bias will be low
- We repeat the cross validation process n times (where n is number of data points) which results in a higher execution time
- This approach leads to higher variation in testing model effectiveness because we test against one data point. So, our estimation gets highly influenced by the data point. If the data point turns out to be an outlier, it can lead to a higher variation

```
Python Code:
from sklearn.model_selection import LeaveOneOut
X = np.array([[1, 2], [3, 4]])
y = np.array([1, 2])
loo = LeaveOneOut()
loo.get_n_splits(X)
for train_index, test_index in loo.split(X):
print("train:", train_index, "validation:", test_index)
X_train, X_test = X[train_index], X[test_index]
y_train, y_test = y[train_index], y[test_index]
R Code:
score = list()
LOOCV_function = function(x,label){
for(i in 1:nrow(x)){
training = x[-i,]
model = #... train model on training
validation = x[i,]
pred = predict(model, validation[,setdiff(names(validation),label)])
score[[i]] = rmse(pred, validation[[label]]) # score/error of ith fold
}
return(unlist(score)) # returns a vector
}
```

LOOCV leaves one data point out. Similarly, you could leave p training examples out to have validation set of size p for each iteration. This is called LPOCV (Leave P Out Cross Validation)

k-fold cross validation

From the above two validation methods, we've learnt:

1. We should train the model on a large portion of the dataset. Otherwise we'll fail to read and recognise the underlying trend in the data. This will eventually result in a higher bias
2. We also need a good ratio of testing data points. As we have seen above, less amount of data points can lead to a variance error while testing the effectiveness of the model
3. We should iterate on the training and testing process multiple times. We should change the train and test dataset distribution. This helps in validating the model effectiveness properly

Do we have a method which takes care of all these 3 requirements?

Yes! That method is known as "k-fold cross validation". It's easy to follow and implement. Below are the steps for it:

1. Randomly split your entire dataset into k"folds"
2. For each k-fold in your dataset, build your model on k – 1 folds of the dataset. Then, test the model to check the effectiveness for *kth* fold
3. Record the error you see on each of the predictions
4. Repeat this until each of the k-folds has served as the test set
5. The average of your k recorded errors is called the cross-validation error and will serve as your performance metric for the model

Below is the visualization of a k-fold validation when k=10.

Now, one of most commonly asked questions is, "How to choose the right value of k?".

Always remember, a lower value of *k* is more biased, and hence undesirable. On the other hand, a higher value of K is less biased, but can suffer from large variability. It is important to know that a smaller value of *k*always takes us towards validation set approach, whereas a higher value of *k* leads to LOOCV approach.

Precisely, LOOCV is equivalent to n-fold cross validation where n is the number of training examples.

Python Code:

```
from sklearn.model_selection import KFold
kf = RepeatedKFold(n_splits=5, n_repeats=10, random_state=None)
for train_index, test_index in kf.split(X):
print("Train:", train_index, "Validation:",test_index)
X_train, X_test = X[train_index], X[test_index]
y_train, y_test = y[train_index], y[test_index]
```

R code:

```
library(caret)
data(iris)
# Define train control for k fold cross validation
train_control <- trainControl(method="cv", number=10)
# Fit Naive Bayes Model
model <- train(Species~., data=iris, trControl=train_control, method="nb")
# Summarise Results
print(model)
```

4. Stratified k-fold cross validation

Stratification is the process of rearranging the data so as to ensure that each fold is a good representative of the whole. For example, in a binary classification problem where each class comprises of 50% of the data, it is best to arrange the data such that in every fold, each class comprises of about half the instances.

It is generally a better approach when dealing with both bias and variance. A randomly selected fold might not adequately represent the minor class, particularly in cases where there is a huge class imbalance.

Python code snippet for stratified k-fold cross validation:

```
from sklearn.model_selection import StratifiedKFold
skf = StratifiedKFold(n_splits=5, random_state=None)
# X is the feature set and y is the target
for train_index, test_index in skf.split(X,y):
print("Train:", train_index, "Validation:", val_index)
X_train, X_test = X[train_index], X[val_index]
y_train, y_test = y[train_index], y[val_index]
```

R Code:

```
library(caret)
# Folds are created on the basis of target variable
folds <- createFolds(factor(data$target), k = 10, list = FALSE)
```

Having said that, if the train set does not adequately represent the entire population, then using a stratified k-fold might not be the best idea. In such cases, one should use a simple k-fold cross validation with repetition.

In repeated cross-validation, the cross-validation procedure is repeated *n* times, yielding *n* random partitions of the original sample. The *n* results are again averaged (or otherwise combined) to produce a single estimation.

Python code for repeated k-fold cross validation:

```
from sklearn.model_selection import RepeatedKFold
rkf = RepeatedKFold(n_splits=5, n_repeats=10, random_state=None)
# X is the feature set and y is the target
for train_index, test_index in rkf.split(X):
print("Train:", train_index, "Validation:", val_index)
X_train, X_test = X[train_index], X[val_index]
y_train, y_test = y[train_index], y[val_index]
```

5. Adversarial Validation

When dealing with real datasets, there are often cases where the test and train sets are very different. As a result, the internal cross-validation techniques might give scores that are not even in the ballpark of the test score. In such cases, adversarial validation offers an interesting solution.

The general idea is to check the degree of similarity between training and tests in terms of feature distribution. If It does not seem to be the case, we can suspect they are quite different. This intuition can be quantified by combining train and test sets, assigning 0/1 labels (0 – train, 1-test) and evaluating a binary classification task.

Let us understand, how this can be accomplished in the below steps:

1. Remove the target variable from the train set

```
train.drop(['target'], axis = 1, inplace = True)
```

2. Create a new target variable which is 1 for each row in the train set, and 0 for each row in the test set

```
train['is_train'] = 1
test['is_train'] = 0
```

3. Combine the train and test datasets

```
df = pd.concat([train, test], axis = 0)
```

4. Using the above newly created target variable, fit a classification model and predict probabilities for each row to be in the test set

```
y = df['is_train']; df.drop('is_train', axis = 1, inplace = True)
# Xgboost parameters
xgb_params = {'learning_rate': 0.05,
'max_depth': 4,
'subsample': 0.9,
'colsample_bytree': 0.9,
'objective': 'binary:logistic',
'silent': 1,
'n_estimators':100,
'gamma':1,
'min_child_weight':4}
```

```
clf = xgb.XGBClassifier(**xgb_params, seed = 10)
```

5. Sort the train set using the calculated probabilities in step 4 and take top n% samples/rows as the validation set (n% is the fraction of the train set you want to keep in the validation set)

```
probs = clf.predict_proba(x1)[:,1]
new_df = pd.DataFrame({'id':train.id, 'probs':probs})
new_df = new_df.sort_values(by = 'probs', ascending=False) # 30% validation set
val_set_ids = new_df.iloc[1:np.int(new_df.shape[0]*0.3),1]
```

val_set_ids will get you the ids from the train set that would constitute the validation set which is most similar to the test set. This will make your validation strategy more robust for cases where the train and test sets are highly dissimilar.

However, you must be careful while using this type of validation technique. Once the distribution of the test set changes, the validation set might no longer be a good subset to evaluate your model on.

6. Cross Validation for time series

Splitting a time-series dataset randomly does not work because the time section of your data will be messed up. For a time series forecasting problem, we perform cross validation in the following manner.

1. Folds for time series cross valdiation are created in a forward chaining fashion
2. Suppose we have a time series for yearly consumer demand for a product during a period of *n* years. The folds would be created like:

```
fold 1: training [1], test [2]
fold 2: training [1 2], test [3]
fold 3: training [1 2 3], test [4]
fold 4: training [1 2 3 4], test [5]
fold 5: training [1 2 3 4 5], test [6]
.
.
.
fold n: training [1 2 3 ..... n-1], test [n]
```

We progressively select a new train and test set. We start with a train set which has a minimum number of observations needed for fitting the model. Progressively, we change our train and test sets with each fold. In most cases, 1 step forecasts might not be very important. In such instances, the forecast origin can be shifted to allow for multi-step errors to be used. For example, in a regression problem, the following code could be used for performing cross validation.

Python Code:

```
from sklearn.model_selection import TimeSeriesSplit
X = np.array([[1, 2], [3, 4], [1, 2], [3, 4]])
y = np.array([1, 2, 3, 4])
tscv = TimeSeriesSplit(n_splits=3)
for train_index, test_index in tscv.split(X):
print("Train:", train_index, "Validation:", val_index)
X_train, X_test = X[train_index], X[val_index]
y_train, y_test = y[train_index], y[val_index]
TRAIN: [0] TEST: [1]
TRAIN: [0 1] TEST: [2]
TRAIN: [0 1 2] TEST: [3]
```

R Code:

```
library(fpp)
library(forecast)
e <- tsCV(ts, Arima(x, order=c(2,0,0), h=1) #CV for arima model
sqrt(mean(e^2, na.rm=TRUE)) # RMSE
```

h = 1 implies that we are taking the error only for 1 step ahead forecasts.

(h =4) 4-step ahead error is depicted in the below diagram. This could be used if you want to evaluate your model for multi-step forecast.

7. Custom Cross Validation Techniques

Unfortunately, there is no single method that works best for all kinds of problem statements. Often, a custom cross validation technique based on a feature, or combination of features, could be created if that gives the user stable cross validation scores while making submissions in hackathons.

For example, in the recently finished contest 'Lord of the Machines' by Analytics Vidhya, the most stable validation technique used by the top finishers was using the campaign *id* variable.

Please have a look at the problem statement and a few approaches discussed by the participants at this thread.

How to measure the model's bias-variance?

After k-fold cross validation, we'll get *k* different model estimation errors (e1, e2 .....ek). In an ideal scenario, these error values should sum up to zero. To return the model's bias, we take the average of all the errors. Lower the average value, better the model.

Similarly for calculating the model variance, we take standard deviation of all the errors. A low value of standard deviation suggests our model does not vary a lot with different subsets of training data.

We should focus on achieving a balance between bias and variance. This can be done by reducing the variance and controlling bias to an extent. It'll result in a better predictive model. This trade-off usually leads to building less complex predictive models as well. For understanding bias-variance trade-off in more depth, please refer to section 9 of this article.

End Notes

In this article, we discussed about overfitting and methods like cross-validation to avoid overfitting. We also looked at different cross-validation methods like validation set approach, LOOCV, k-fold cross validation, stratified k-fold and so on, followed by each approach's implementation in Python and R performed on the Iris dataset.

Printed by Libri Plureos GmbH in Hamburg,
Germany